D0983341

AN ELEMENTARY APPROACH
TO THINKING UNDER UNCERTAINTY

AN ELEMENTARY APPROACH
TO THINKING UNDER UNCERTAINTY

Ruth Beyth-Marom & Shlomith Dekel

Ruth Gombo & Moshe Shaked

Translated and adapted from the Hebrew by

Sarah Lichtenstein,
Benny Marom,
& Ruth Beyth-Marom

LEA LAWRENCE ERLBAUM ASSOCIATES, PUBLISHERS
1985   Hillsdale, New Jersey   London

Lawrence Erlbaum Associates, Inc., Publishers
365 Broadway
Hillsdale, New Jersey 07642

Library of Congress Cataloging in Publication Data
Main entry under title:

An Elementary approach to thinking under uncertainty.

  Bibliography: p.
  Includes index.
  1. Uncertainty.   2. Thought and thinking.   3. Intuition
(Psychology) I. Beyth-Marom, Ruth.   II. Lichtenstein,
Sarah.   III. Marom, Benny.
BF463.U5E43 1985   153.4′2   85-4427
ISBN 0-89859-379-4

Printed in the United States of America
10 9 8 7 6 5 4 3 2 1

Contents

Preface

Between 1974 and 1980, a group of scientists and educators at the University of Jerusalem in Israel developed and wrote a textbook, in Hebrew, called *Thinking Under Uncertainty*.[1] That text is now used in a course taught to Israeli fourteen-year-olds, to improve their probabilistic thinking skills, introduce concepts like *uncertainty,* point out circumstances under which our thinking processes lead us astray, and suggest some tools to improve our skills when dealing with uncertainty.

The present book presents a translation of the Hebrew text, rewritten to include material more suited to American adults than to Israeli school children.[2] However, the elementary approach used in the original is retained here. Although the topic of uncertainty is an advanced topic within mathematics, this book should be accessible to any adult with a minimal knowledge of arithmetic, that is, addition, subtraction, multiplication, division, and the calculation of percentages.

[1]The Hebrew text was developed and prepared within the framework of the Center for Teaching of Humanities and Social Sciences of the School of Education, the Hebrew University, Jerusalem, in cooperation with the Curriculum Center, the Ministry of Education and Culture, Israel. The rights of the Hebrew version are preserved to the Curriculum Center of the Israeli Ministry of Education and Culture and they cannot be partly or wholly transferred to anyone.

[2]Funds for the translation and adaptation were provided by the U.S. Army Research Institute for the Behavioral and Social Sciences under Contract MDA903-81-C-0376 to Decision Research, a Branch of Perceptronics, Inc. The views, opinions, and findings contained in this book are those of the authors and should not be construed as an official Department of the Army position, policy, or decision.

The primary encouragement for the development of a curriculum on thinking under uncertainty — of which this book is one product — came from two people: Dr. Daniel Kahneman, a research psychologist who studies people's thinking processes, and Dr. Seymour Fox, former Head of the School of Education at the Hebrew University, Jerusalem. Both of these men seek the incorporation of scientific (educational and psychological) ideas into school curricula.

Other contributors to the Hebrew text are Baruch Fischhoff and Sarah Lichtenstein, who reviewed the text and made suggestions, and Miriam Basok and Efrat Balberg, who were helpful in the first stages of planning and writing. Finally, we learned much from a number of junior high school teachers who had the courage to teach *Thinking Under Uncertainty* long before the textbook was ready: Yossi Leshem, Judith Miller, Aliza Peer, Tamar Kahn, and Lea Shatil. We deeply thank all these people; without their help, the raw ideas would never have developed into a textbook.

The present book was prepared during the first author's visit to Decision Research, a Branch of Perceptronics, in Eugene, Oregon. We are grateful to the people at Decision Research, Paul Slovic, Baruch Fischhoff, Don Mac-Gregor, Nancy Collins, and Geri Hanson, for their warm support, advice, and typing and drafting skills.

Our special thanks go to Benny Marom for his translation and to Sarah Lichtenstein, who combined her editing and writing skills with her knowledge and understanding of the field to help adapt the book for an adult American audience.

Introduction

When you start reading this book, you don't know much about it. What is it about? Will you understand it? Will you enjoy it? About all these questions you experience feelings of uncertainty. This is just one example of the uncertainties that accompany nearly every step of our lives.

We feel uncertain about the small events in our lives:

> When will the bus arrive?
> Will it rain tomorrow?
> Can I stick to my diet this week?

And about more major problems:

> Can I get a good job?
> Should I marry this person?
> Will I survive the surgical operation?

Businesses and other groups of people also face uncertainty:

> Will this new product sell?
> Will our research be funded?
> Is the defendant guilty as charged?

Even the largest organizations in our society experience uncertainty:

> Will a tax cut fuel inflation?
> Will a hard stance on defense decrease the chances of war?

But uncertainty does not prevent us from making decisions. We must decide whether or not to carry an umbrella before we know for sure what the weather will be. Legislators must vote yes or no (or abstain from voting) on a tax-cut bill even if they are not certain of its effects. Nearly every step we take, whether as private citizens, as groups, or as a whole society, is the result of a decision made under uncertainty.

Thousands of years ago, people tried to solve uncertainty by consulting the prophets. The prophets exchanged uncertainty for certainty; they told people what would happen in the future as if it were certain. Even today, people go to astrologers, look at horoscopes, and take other actions that give one the feeling of diminishing or eliminating uncertainty.

Most people, however, don't try to eliminate all uncertainty. They live with it with the help of their *intuition*. Intuition is a kind of sensation or inner feeling that guides us and shows us how to act. It is a personal thinking tool that we use without asking how it really functions. Intuition comes from one's life experiences; thus, it varies from person to person.

Researchers have realized how important it is to look at the way people live with, or in spite of, uncertainty. They have tried to find out how our intuitions work, and how people think and act in uncertain situations. The results of this research indicate that, despite the personal nature of intuition, there are strong communalities among the intuitions of different people when they think under uncertainty. The young and the elderly, professionals and lay-people, all use similar thinking processes. When these processes were compared to the best known methods for treating uncertainty—methods taken from statistics, probability, and decision theory—researchers found that our intuitive thinking processes were much simpler. Although these simpler methods are often satisfactory, they can sometimes lead us into errors. Consider the following example:

> Susan has just been admitted to the hospital in labor. The doctor on duty tells Susan that the last six babies born there were girls. "In that case," Susan responded, "I figure I'll have a boy."

Many people would answer as Susan did, some of them with a smile, others with great seriousness. In such situations, our intuition tells us that things "balance out," so that a series of consecutive births of girls will make a boy more likely for the next birth. But here our intuition leads us astray. More careful thought makes us realize that the gender of those other six babies cannot possibly influence or change the gender of Susan's baby. This is just one example of a bias in our intuition that can, in other circumstances, have an enormous influence on human behavior.

This book presents an introduction to uncertainty based on research about people's intuitions. It describes how people usually think about uncertainty and the errors these intuitive modes of thought can produce. It offers some better ways to think about uncertainty.

We are not trying to change your intuitions. Indeed, even the intuitions of researchers who have been working in this domain for many years haven't drastically changed. Instead, our goals are to alert you to situations in which intuition can lead you astray and to provide you with new ways of thinking clearly in those situations.

We have included some practice exercises at the end of most chapters. There are no answers provided, but we hope you will try the exercises as a way of deepening your understanding of the topic. Your real learning will come, however, when you apply the techniques and ways of thinking described here to your own life and to the uncertainties you face every day.

We are not prophets or astrologers. We can't convert uncertainty into certainty, nor can we provide absolute solutions. The techniques recommended herein carry no guarantee that you will achieve desired outcomes in uncertain situations. But using these techniques should produce better outcomes more often than not using them.

This book is divided into three sections. The first section, Chapters 1–4, provides a general framework for thinking about uncertainty. The second section, Chapters 5–7, discusses some tools that are frequently used in dealing with problems under uncertainty. The last section, Chapters 8–11, deals specifically with probability assessment.

I A GENERAL FRAMEWORK

1 Certainty and Uncertainty

1.1 FEELINGS OF CERTAINTY AND UNCERTAINTY

We often hear, as part of the answer to a question, phrases like "I'm sure that...," "I've no doubt that...," or "I'm positive that...." People using these phrases really believe that they have the answer to the question and feel no doubt in its truthfulness.

—Question: What are you doing right now?
  Answer: I am reading.
  Nobody would ask, "Are you sure about that?"
—Question: David, what gender are you?
  Answer: I'm sure I'm a man.
—Question: Elizabeth, what will you do this afternoon?
  Answer: No doubt about it, I'll go to the movies.
—Question: John, whose picture is that?
  Answer: I'm confident that's my sister.
—Question: Dan, what kind of sandwich did you eat for lunch today?
  Answer: I know for certain I had a cheese sandwich.

In all these examples, the question asked relates to a fact or to an event in the past, present, or future. The person answering feels very certain, very confident, with no doubt at all. David is *sure;* Elizabeth has *no doubt;* John is *confident;* and Dan knows *for certain.*

3

> We experience certainty about a specific question when we
> have a feeling of complete belief or complete confidence in a
> single answer to the question.

Certainty feelings originate from the confidence we have in our
knowledge, in the experiences we have accumulated through the years (Dan
has seen and tasted cheese many times and he knows what it looks like and
how it tastes), and in the confidence we have in the functioning of our
senses (Dan relied on his eyesight and taste).

This confidence may sometimes fail us. Elizabeth, who is so sure what her
plans are for the afternoon, may find such a long line at the theater that she
has no chance to get in. She just didn't think about such a possibility
beforehand.

Knowledge and experience generally fail us when we face radically new
developments. Until the 15th century, people were certain that the sun
revolved around the earth. But some of those who heard of Copernicus's
new ideas about planetary motion replaced their previous certainty with
doubt.

Our senses can also fail us. Have you ever sat in a standing train as
another train began to move? Sometimes you get the strong sensation that it
is your own train that is moving. Only after the moving train has passed
your window do you realize that your train is still standing in the same
place. Novice mountain climbers often misjudge the summit, believing they
are on the final approach when in fact they are still far away. As with our
experiences, we cannot always rely on our senses. They can fail us in many
situations.

In spite of these occasional failures, we do rely on our senses and the
knowledge and experience that we have accumulated, because most of the
time, they work. Moreover, if we had to make the effort to think about each
step we take each time we take it, we wouldn't be able to function at all.
Should we stop eating just because there is a small chance that the food in
front of us is not the food we think it is? We prefer assuming that our
knowledge and our senses are good enough.

In contrast to the feelings of certainty we experience with some questions,
there are other questions that lead us to feel uncertain.

Will it rain next Saturday?

Are there intelligent creatures in outer space?

Will the strike be settled within a week?

Where have I met this person before?

How many traffic accidents were there last year?

Concerning such questions, some of us, and sometimes all of us, feel uncertainty. To some questions, we can't offer even one plausible answer. Who ruled Italy in 1563? Most people will be unable to suggest even one possible answer.

For other questions, many answers come to mind; some seem more suitable than others, but we do not feel completely confident about any one answer. How many members are there in the U.S. House of Representatives? I think it may be 435, but it might be 235, or 436, and so on. My confidence is spread over a large number of possible answers.

Consider an archeologist digging a site in the Great Plains of North America who wants to determine the date at which people lived at the site. While digging, she finds a leaf-shaped flint implement that she uses as a clue for deciding about the date of the site. She knows that such flints are prehistoric. Furthermore, its shape rules out some periods in prehistory but leaves two possibilities: (1) the present implement is most typical of the "Clovis" type of projectile point, which was used between 9000 and 8000 B.C.; therefore, it is *highly probable* that the site dates to that period. (2) However, the point has some characteristics of the "Folsom" type, which was in use later, between 8000 and 7000 B.C.; thus, it *may be* from that period. Moreover, such prehistoric points are highly valued by collectors and a ready market for modern fakes has developed. This point might be a fake. Thus, (3) *perhaps* the site is modern.

The archeologist is sure that these three possibilities cover the range of possibilities. Other possibilities do not seem plausible. She has three possible answers to the question. She feels a *partial belief* in each of the three answers. This partial belief is expressed in the words "highly probable," "may be," and "perhaps." At that moment, there is no one answer about which she feels complete confidence. Therefore, we say that the archeologist feels uncertain about the question "How old is the site?"

To summarize: We experience uncertainty concerning a specific question when we have a partial belief in each of a number of possible answers to the question.

But what about when we can't think of even one plausible answer to a question, as in the example of the ruler of Italy in 1563? Although we don't have a partial belief in a number of answers (because we can't think of any answers), we do feel uncertainty. If someone were to present us with a number of possible answers, we wouldn't feel complete confidence in any of them. In order to include this last case, in which we can't think of even one answer, in the definition of uncertainty, we define the feeling of uncertainty negatively:

> We experience uncertainty about a specific question when we can't give a single answer with complete confidence.

Exercises for Section 1.1

1. Sometimes in hindsight, we find out that our certainty feelings were not justified. Think about ways in which one's certainty feelings could be unjustified, for each of the following situations:

(a) I attended a concert yesterday.
(b) I've been here before.
(c) The store I'm looking for is right around the corner.
(d) My watch indicates that it's eight o'clock.
(e) It is now eight p.m.
(f) I am standing in front of my house.
(g) I will write a letter after the guests leave.

2. Think of at least three times when you were sure about something, but turned out to be wrong.

1.2 CHARACTERISTICS OF UNCERTAINTY FEELINGS

Personal and general uncertainty. There are some questions for which we feel that uncertainty is currently unavoidable. These are questions towards which we feel that *nobody* now knows the right answer.

Is there any sort of life on other stars?

Is there a monster in Lake Ness in Scotland?

I am about to toss a coin. Will it come up heads or tails?

How did Shubert intend to finish his "Unfinished Symphony"?

For some of these questions, we expect that a certain answer will be known in the future. As soon as I toss the coin, I'll know whether it came up heads or tails. Other questions may be unresolved forever. Since Shubert died before he finished his last symphony (and left no notes), we'll never know his intentions for it.

In contrast to questions about which uncertainty feelings are unavoidable, there are questions that, in principle, somebody can answer with certainty. In which hand am I hiding a coin? You feel uncertainty but I don't. I'm not sure how many Representatives there are in Congress, but I recognize that other people know the answer with certainty.

When a person feels that, in principle, there is now no certain answer to a question, then that person feels *general uncertainty*.

When a person feels uncertainty concerning the question but realizes that, in principle, one could feel certainty, that person feels *personal uncertainty*.

Sometimes we may be more comfortable with general uncertainty, because we can't blame it on our own ignorance. On the other hand, with personal uncertainty we have the hope that we can resolve the uncertainty by consulting a more knowledgeable source.

Amounts of uncertainty.   Paul was asked, "What is the longest river in the U.S.? He answered with complete confidence, "the Mississippi."[1] Next he was asked, "What is the longest river in the world?" This time, he felt uncertain. He was then given a hint: The answer is one of the four rivers: Mississippi, Yangtze, Amazon, or Nile.[2] Let us now consider four possible states of mind Paul might be in after receiving the hint.

A. Paul thinks all the answers are equally likely.
B. Now that Paul sees the four possibilities, he remembers reading about Egypt not long ago; the article stated that the Nile is the longest river in the world.

Those two situations are extreme ones in the sense that the first one represents maximum uncertainty (every possibility is seen as equally likely) and the second represents certainty. Between those two situations there are many intermediate situations; each of them reflects different amounts of uncertainty.

C. Paul decides that the Yangtze is certainly not the right answer, but among the three remaining (Mississippi, Amazon, and Nile), he has no preference. In this case, he feels less uncertainty than in the first situation, in which he had no preference among four answers.
D. Paul thinks the answer is the Amazon, but he isn't certain about it. He judges the answers Mississippi and Nile as equally likely, but not as likely as the Amazon. He is sure that the Yangtze is wrong.

---

[1]By "the Mississippi" we mean the entire river system that includes the Mississippi, the Missouri, and the Red Rock.
[2]Mississippi: 3710 miles; Yangtze: 3400 miles; Amazon: 4000 miles; Nile: 4145 miles.

We can now order the four situations according to the amount of Paul's uncertainty. He is most uncertain in situation A, because he feels no preference among the four answers. The next most uncertain situation is C; he feels no preferences among three of the answers. Paul also reduced the set of possible answers to three in D, but here he feels that one is more likely than the other two. This uneven distribution of confidence in D makes D less uncertain than C, where he thought all three were equally likely. Case B, of course, is the least uncertain; Paul feels no uncertainty at all.

The amount of uncertainty depends on two factors: The number of possible answers one can give and the strength of preference one has for each answer relative to the others.

---

(1) If all possible answers seem equally likely, then the more possible answers there are, the more uncertainty we feel.

(2) When there are a fixed number of possible answers, the amount of uncertainty depends on the spread of confidence across the possible answers. We feel most uncertainty when all answers are equally likely. As the spread of confidence across the set of answers becomes less uniform, we feel less uncertainty. At the extreme, when we are completely confident in one answer, our uncertainty is eliminated.

The first rule above may be exemplified by comparing one's feelings of uncertainty just before rolling a fair die and just before tossing a coin. There is more uncertainty with the die than with the coin because the die has six possible outcomes while the coin has only two.

The second rule above may be exemplified by comparing one's feelings of uncertainty about the roll of a fair die with the roll of shaved die, one on which a six appears more often than any of the other numbers. There is more uncertainty with the fair die because all sides are equally likely to be rolled.

We are not speaking about some abstract notion of "objective uncertainty," that exists as a characteristic "out there" in the world. Rather, we are speaking about subjective feelings, beliefs, or sensations. Those feelings are naturally very personal and depend on experience, knowledge, and other individual characteristics. One can feel uncertain about who invented the telescope, feeling that it was either Kepler or Galileo. One's feelings of uncertainty will increase if the names Copernicus and Newton, as plausible additional answers, come to mind.

Whether one is dealing with general uncertainty or personal uncertainty, the amount of uncertainty may be different from person to person. Two people may experience different degrees of uncertainty because they have different numbers of possible answers to the same question (as with the question about the invention of the telescope, above) or because they have different distributions of uncertainty across the same number of possible answers. Do flying saucers exist? People differ in their beliefs about this; they differ in the amount of confidence they place on each of the two possible answers, yes and no, and thus in their overall uncertainty.

Changes in amount of uncertainty. Feelings of uncertainty aren't necessarily constant. Sometimes the amount of uncertainty changes; one feels more uncertain or less uncertain because of additional information about the question. More information can change the amount of uncertainty either because the new information adds to or diminishes the number of possible answers or because it changes the relative amount of confidence that one attaches to each of the possible answers. Consider the following example:

A. Susan has just finished reading a murder mystery and knows that X is the murderer.

B. Susan then gives the book to Henry. On the first page, there is a list of the names of all the characters in the book, one of whom is the murderer. Henry has no idea who that might be because he hasn't read the book yet. Therefore, he considers all of them equally likely.

C. Henry then reads the first 100 pages. He now believes with near certainty that X is the murderer.

D. James also reads the first 100 pages of the book. He also suspects X, but he is less sure about it. He is less confident than Henry because he thinks that Y might also be the murderer.

E. Henry then reads all but the last six pages of the book. He still thinks X could be the murderer, but he is now less certain than he was after reading only the first 100 pages. Because the author has presented so many conflicting clues, he now feels that except for the murdered person (it was a murder and not a suicide), every one of the people mentioned at the beginning of the book might be the murderer.

This example shows that:

1. Concerning a single question such as, "Who is the murderer?" different people can feel different amounts of uncertainty. Comparing A with B (Susan has read it and Henry hasn't), we see that Susan knows for sure who the murderer is, but Henry has no idea. He feels uncertain about the question.

2. Adding information (by reading part of the book) may decrease the uncertainty one feels (compare B with C), increase uncertainty (compare C with E), or not change it at all (compare B with E). One can reach the same amount of uncertainty in one case because of ignorance (B: Henry hadn't read the book at all) and in another case because of a lot of inconsistent information (E: Henry when he had nearly finished the book).

3. The same data can influence different people differently. Compare James in D with Henry in C. They feel different amounts of confidence toward the answer "X is the murderer" although they have the same information.

Exercises for Section 1.2

1. For each question, do you think the uncertainty is general or personal?

(a) How many microbes are there in the world?
(b) Is the number 247,719 divisible by 7?
(c) If I had bought a lottery ticket yesterday, would I have won?
(d) Which athlete will win the race?
(e) What is the age of the earth?
(f) How much money does George have in his pocket?

2. Think of three examples of questions for which you have personal feelings of uncertainty and three questions for which you have general feelings of uncertainty.

3. Each of the following questions has two possible answers, yes and no. For each question:

(a) Think of a piece of information that will *decrease* your uncertainty by making you more sure that you know the right answer.
(b) Think of another piece of information that will *increase* your uncertainty relative to the uncertainty you felt after (a). This information will in some way contradict the information you gave in (a).

(1) Will tomorrow be a nice day?
(2) Is milk good for health?
(3) Should children be taught to read before entering first grade?
(4) Will the Republicans win the next election?
(5) Is my car about to break down?
(6) Will Nancy remember to pick me up at 5:00 p.m.?
(7) Will the alarm go off tomorrow morning?
(8) Will I impress the interviewer during my job interview?

1.3 UNCERTAINTY AND DECISION MAKING

In everyday situations, the uncertainty we feel usually doesn't keep us from acting. Even the most cautious of us doesn't delay action until feeling certain. If one always waited until one felt certain, one would rarely take any action at all.

It is not certain that I'll reach work without an accident on the way.

I can't be certain that when I turn on the hot water I won't get a cold shower.

I can't even be completely certain when I go to bed at night that the bed won't collapse.

When such possibilities are raised, we are suddenly conscious that all those situations are, to some extent, uncertain. But the chance of something going wrong is so small that we are willing to take the chance and proceed to drive to work, turn on the shower, or climb into bed.

Even when we are not willing to disregard the less probable outcomes, we do not always avoid action. Sometimes we can act and take suitable safety steps.

I'll take an umbrella on a cloudy day because I don't want to get wet if it rains.

My friends said that they will try to visit me tonight. I'm chilling a bottle of wine, although I know that they probably won't come.

In contrast to these examples in which we act because the uncertainty is small or the safety steps are easy, there are situations in which uncertainty looms large. Still we must take some action.

How much food should I prepare for the party?

What job shall I accept?

With decisions that are important to us, we act, but only after careful consideration, and often still very much in doubt.

Finally, remember that not making a decision is itself a kind of decision; not taking an action is a kind of action.

Shall I go to a movie tonight? I have read conflicting reviews of the film and feel uncertain about whether I'll like it. At 9 p.m. I realize that it's too late to decide, since the movie has already started.

This book looks at situations in which people feel uncertainty. We discuss mistakes that we and others make when thinking about uncertainty. We suggest how to detect fallacies and biases and how to avoid them. In general, we explore how we can improve our thought processes and our thinking under uncertainty.

But even if we could consistently adopt all the recommendations made herein, we can't be sure that each rational and carefully considered decision will lead to the desired result. If we decide at the end of a careful consideration, during which we avoid every possible fallacy and bias, to choose job A over job B, job A may still turn out to be a much worse job than job B. In this case, although we adopted a good thinking process and made a good decision, we got a poor result.

This is a natural characteristic of situations in which we feel uncertain: The outcomes of our decisions are not predictable in advance. Our capacity to predict an outcome in advance is the factor that distinguishes decisions under certainty from decisions under uncertainty.

It is August. A mountain guide has to decide when to start a group trek. It is important for the guide to go early in the morning, but not before the sun rises. Because of reasons related to the availability of the vehicle and its driver, the guide finds out that there are only two possible starting times, 3 a.m. or 6 a.m. The guide has no doubt. At 3 a.m., the sun certainly isn't up. At 6 a.m. it certainly is. The guide decides without any difficulty to begin the trip at 6 a.m. and feels certain about the outcome of the decision. These thought and decision processes are good, and the result was the desired one: the sun has indeed risen by 6 a.m.

This characteristic, that a good decision process will lead to a desired outcome, is characteristic of situations in which we feel justified certainty. In contrast to such situations, there are situations in which we feel uncertainty. We can't predict, in advance, what the outcomes will be; therefore, we can't be sure that a good decision process will certainly lead to the desired results.

The guide later had to decide whether to take Route A or Route B. The goal was to reach the lake as quickly as possible. The guide knew that Route A is shorter than Route B and that the routes have similar, unpaved roads. The guide decided to go the shortest way, Route A. However, close to the lake, the group found that Route A was completely blocked by a rock slide; they had to retrace their steps and take Route B.

If someone had asked the guide, "Are you absolutely certain that taking Route A will get you to the lake faster than Route B?" the response would have been "No, not absolutely certain, but pretty sure." Unexpected things can happen. No one could be completely confident that Route A was clear, but one couldn't be completely confident that Route B was clear either. This is a characteristic situation in making decisions under uncertainty. There was nothing wrong with the decision processes of the guide. According to the data available, the guide made a good decision, but the outcome was bad. Because of an unexpected rock slide, the road was blocked and the group arrived at the lake past sunset.

We have seen that a good decision made under uncertainty can lead to an undesired result. In contrast, consider this:

> An Israeli visited the United States. When he came out of the airport, he hailed a cab. The driver looked at him and said, "Are you an Israeli?" The man was surprised, saying, "Yes, I'm an Israeli; how did you know?" The driver answered, "That's easy. You wear a patch on your eye. Moshe Dayan also wore a patch on his eye. Dayan was Israeli. So I figured you are, too."

Poor decision processes can sometimes lead to good results.

When we feel certain about a specific situation, we can predict with complete confidence the outcome of each of our possible actions.

When we feel any uncertainty about a situation, we can't predict with complete confidence what the outcomes of our actions will be.

Under justified certainty, good decision processes are followed by desired results, but under uncertainty, good decision processes can sometimes be followed by undesired results and poor decision processes can sometimes be followed by desired results.

Because of these characteristics of decisions under uncertainty, there is no way to make inferences about the quality of the decision process based on the quality of the results. You can't tell the guide "because you are late, your decision to take Route A was wrong." This argument would be as unreasonable as saying "you didn't get six when you threw the dice; therefore, you didn't throw well."

It would be reasonable to ask, "If I can't be certain of getting a desired result, why should I try to improve my decision processes?" The answer is that the better our decision processes are, the more *likely* good results are. Someone who adopts good decision processes gets *more* desired results than someone who adopts bad decision processes.

The rules and suggestions presented in this book are recommendations for good thought processes to use when making decisions under uncertainty. The overriding message from them is "Wait a minute. Think twice. Don't rush to conclusions." To adopt these techniques takes much time and effort. Not all problems, situations, or questions that arise under uncertainty will require special efforts. But if you know the rules for better thinking, you can use them for problems that are specially important to you.

Exercises for Section 1.3

1. For each of the following decisions, first judge whether the decision was good or bad. Then, for each bad decision, think of a possible good outcome. For each good decision, think of a possible bad outcome.

(a) Last night Bill decided that he wouldn't set his alarm clock but would wake up by himself.
(b) This morning, Bill refused to eat an egg that was bought three weeks ago; instead, he cooked an egg that was bought yesterday.
(c) Bill left the house by jumping out a window, although his apartment is on the second floor.
(d) When Bill got to the bus stop, two buses arrived. He took the full bus, saying to himself, "full buses get there faster because they make fewer stops."
(e) When he arrived at his college, he was late to class. He entered another class, saying "I have to make life more interesting."
(f) Bill had a dentist appointment at 2 p.m. He arrived there at 1:45, saying, "I don't want any more trouble today."
(g) The minute he got home, he sat down to study for his exams, saying to himself, "I still feel pretty good. Later this evening I'll feel too tired to study."
(h) In the evening he went to visit a friend he hadn't seen in a long time.
(i) He walked back home, saying to himself, "The bus schedule at night is terrible. Sometimes you have to wait an hour for a bus."
(j) Before going to sleep, he set his alarm for 7 a.m., saying to himself, "I have to learn from experience."

2. Think of five examples of good decisions that may be followed by undesired results.

2 Defining the Uncertain Situation

2.1 INTRODUCTION

"On the first of January, 1981, Wilma A. Smith, 'the lessor' will transfer to 'the lessee,' George S. Jones, the house keys for the residence at 1850 Main Street, Parkington, Illinois." This sentence from a legal contract is formulated clearly and accurately. The words, "lessor," "lessee," and "residence" are explicitly identified. Every word in the sentence has one and only one meaning and the whole sentence portrays a clear message.

This strictness does not usually exist in our natural language; our everyday language is not built in such an exact fashion. Everyday language, because of its many uses, includes many words whose meanings are not clear. Even two people who know the language will not always take the same meaning from a single sentence. For example, a husband and wife are arguing: "Was last year's vacation a success?" One says, "We visited too many cities and got exhausted; the vacation was not successful." The other counters, "We got to see new parts of the country; it was terrific."

This situation is one that could be characterized as a certainty situation. The vacation is over and both people know the facts about it. The argument is not about the facts but about the meaning of the term "successful." The difference in the meaning of terms is important in situations involving certainty. We will see that agreement on the meaning of the terms is even more important in uncertain situations.

Suppose the argument took place before the vacation. Will the coming vacation be successful? This is an uncertain situation because no one knows how the vacation will actually turn out. Differences of opinion will exist, and the debate will concern facts about possible future events, but in addition to that, part of the debate will involve a lack of agreement on the meaning of "a successful vacation." Uncertain situations cause difficulties because of their very nature. In order not to make it even harder to cope with these situations, one has to be meticulous about the definitions. Defining terms is actually the first stage in looking clearly at problems; therefore, a clear formulation of the problem is many times the key to good decisions and efficient actions.

In this chapter, we hope to convince you of the importance of clear formulation in general and in uncertain situations in particular. We also recommend a tool that will enable you to test whether a problem is formulated clearly.

2.2 VAGUENESS AND AMBIGUITY IN LANGUAGE

If we ask for an opinion about a mutual friend and get the answer "nice," we will not learn much about her character or her appearance. There are many words in our vocabulary like "nice," "successful," "difficult," or "bad," that point out the speaker's general intention without communicating much information. In daily life, we infer the exact meaning behind such general words and phrases with the help of past knowledge about the circumstances or past acquaintance with the speaker. For example, when Joseph tells John, "What a nice day," John can interpret it as "the sea was quiet; it was not hot; nothing went wrong with the boat," because the two of them just came back from a day of sailing. For someone returning from a tiring trip, "a nice day" might mean lying down on the sofa reading a book and drinking beer.

> Vague words convey only a general meaning that we make specific with the help of past knowledge and the context in which they are said.

There are other words in the language that convey a relatively exact meaning, but each such word has several possible meanings. Consider the following example:

1. She wore a hard rock (diamond) on her ring finger.
2. This is hard rock candy.
3. Drilling through hard rock.
4. My favorite kind of music is hard rock.
5. This rocking chair gives a hard rock.

Every one of the meanings is understandable in its context. In a suitable context there is no vagueness about it. We call such words ambiguous.

> Ambiguous words are words with multiple meanings.

The advantages of vagueness and ambiguity.   There are many domains in which vagueness or ambiguity in natural language is a positive contribution. A good example is the symbolic language of literature. The poet David Fogel has described his childhood as "blue." He did not intend to provide an exact definition of his childhood. Instead, in the phrase "blue childhood" he tried to convey general sensations concerning his childhood: blue sea, blue sky, peacefulness. Blue also evokes thoughts of inner sadness or even of puritanism ("blue laws"). But this list of possible meanings does not exhaust the possibilities. The poet and the reader can find a broader and deeper meaning to the expression "blue childhood." The poet chooses or even invents vague or ambiguous words and expressions; the more such expressions, the richer the poem.

Another use of vague language that all of us take for granted is not the language that makes a poem rich metaphorically, but makes the writer rich materialistically. This is advertising language: "Things go better with Coke," "Marlboro Country," or "Reach out and touch someone." With vague and ambiguous expressions, the writer tries to influence the listener without the listener's awareness of the ambiguity.

In daily life, we sometimes use vague or ambiguous language to avoid conflict or to be polite. If somebody asks us "What happened to Fred? Why isn't he in your office any more?", we may prefer to answer, "It didn't work out," rather than going into detail with "Fred got fired because he came late, quarreled with others, and was even suspected of dipping into the till." By saying "It didn't work out," we leave the meaning intentionally ambiguous. In daily conversation, a really specific answer would often sound ridiculous. For example, "How are you?" Only a nut would answer in detail about body temperature, a lingering cough, recent mood changes, and so on.

Even in formal language, ambiguity and vagueness are sometimes used intentionally. In the peace settlement between Egypt and Israel, there was mention of future talks about autonomy with reference to the Palestinian problem. But autonomy for what or whom? This was left unspecified so that in discussing the treaty, Begin could say the autonomy referred to the Palestinian *people* while Sadat could say it referred to the disputed *land*.

To summarize: there are many advantages to vague and ambiguous expressions in natural language.

> Vague or ambiguous expressions can: (a) activate the listener's imagination; (b) conceal information; or (c) avoid conflict.

The disadvantages of vagueness and ambiguity. The trouble comes when we use vague and ambiguous expressions unintentionally or unnecessarily. A vague formulation of a message may cause misunderstanding, wrong decisions, or faulty interpretations. Most of us remember saying "I didn't intend to insult you; you simply didn't understand me" or "That's not what I meant at all." After a long argument, we hear "Ah, is that what you're driving at? I agree completely." Vagueness causes misunderstanding because of the gap between the meaning the speaker intends and the meaning the listener is getting.

Henry claims that during the last 2000 years humans have not progressed. Helen claims that humans have made astonishing progress. The debate between the two relies on the meaning of "progress." Henry means moral progress; he doesn't see any. Helen means technological progress, which obviously has occurred.

Dan and Paul are discussing the need for a Saturday committee meeting. Dan says, "we have to start early because the agenda is so long." Paul says, "No, I like to sleep in on Saturday. Let's start late." Will they have a rancorous fight and cancel the meeting without ever discovering that Dan's "early" on a Saturday is 9:30 a.m., which is also Paul's "late"?

As a first step in any argument, the two sides must test the terms. Do they understand each other? Do they agree on the interpretation of critical terms? When each one of those taking part in an argument means something else by the same term, they will not argue *with* one another, but in parallel.

The debate over human progress in the last 2000 years should begin by reaching an agreement concerning the subject. Even after an agreement that the topic is "moral progress," debate may continue. Helen can argue that eliminating the death penalty means moral progress, whereas Henry claims that it is a retreat. But this is a debate about substantive values, not a debate based on misunderstanding.

> Vague terms cause misunderstanding.
>
> Early agreement should be reached on the definition of terms.
>
> A debate after such agreement may be fruitful and interesting.
>
> A debate based on vague and ambiguous terms is pointless and unproductive.

Exercises for Section 2.2

1. Find in the newspaper or any piece of literature ten examples of intentional vagueness.
2. Look at a weekly horoscope.

    a. Find the vague or ambiguous words.
    b. Write a new horoscope replacing each vague or ambiguous word with a clear one.
    c. Did you learn something about horoscopes?

2.3 THE CLAIRVOYANCE TEST

When we are in an uncertain situation and we can't decide between a number of possible answers to a question or problem, we must first clearly define the problem with which we are faced. How will we know when the problem is clearly defined?

A test for determining clarity is the "clairvoyance test." Imagine a person who knows the answers to all possible questions. This person is called the "clairvoyant." The clairvoyant knows all that happened in the past, all that happens in the present, and all that will happen in the future. But the clairvoyant knows only facts and cannot make interpretations or inferences.

The clairvoyant knows all facts but does not explain, interpret, or infer.

A term, phrase, or statement passes the clairvoyance test if the clairvoyant, relying solely on facts, is able to say whether the statement is true or false.

A question passes the clairvoyance test if the clairvoyant, relying solely on facts, can answer it.

---

1. How many people will attend the lecture?
2. Will the audience be large or small?

The clairvoyant can easily answer the first question: "One hundred forty-three people will attend the lecture." The clairvoyant will not be able to answer the second question because it is not clear whether 143 people is a large audience or a small audience.

A local group is sponsoring a public debate on creationism versus evolutionism in the public schools. Two members of the group want to decide whether it will be a "hot debate." The importance of a clear definition may be seen if we assume that such a debate has already taken place, that the two of them were present, but that they can't agree whether the debate was hot or not. One says it was a hot debate because it went twenty minutes over the scheduled time. The other one claims that it was not a hot debate because the discussants were all polite to the last. How could they define "hot debate" to avoid this disagreement? A hot debate could be defined as "a debate that lasts long after the scheduled time." This definition would not pass the clairvoyance test, because the clairvoyant would not know how many minutes or hours "long after" meant. Definitions like "The debate lasted more than two hours" or "At least two discussants raised their voices above 30 decibels for at least ten seconds" would probably pass the clairvoyance test. After the debate any one of these definitions could be used to decide whether it was a hot debate.

Will my two friends become reconciled? The phrase "become reconciled" must be defined before this question can pass the clairvoyance test. We could define it as "My two friends will say hello to each other when they next meet," or as "One of them will invite the other to dinner within the next month." Either of these definitions would pass the clairvoyance test.

Of course, saying hello is not really all that is meant by "becoming reconciled." Often a definition that passes the clairvoyance test will be much narrower than the ordinary meaning of a phrase. One way to broaden the definition is to list several specific behaviors, any one of which would be taken as indicating reconciliation: "They say hello next time they meet *or* one invites the other to dinner within the next month *or* they talk together on the phone at least once within the next month." This definition is broader but still passes the clairvoyance test. Even so, such definitions do not capture the subjective feelings of friendship and affection that reconciliation implies. Clear definitions that pass the clairvoyance test will not always contain all the rich implications and associations of ordinary language. But the clarity that the clairvoyance test assures is necessary for effective decision making.

> For effective decision making, all terms in the problem
> statement should be defined so that they pass the clairvoyance
> test.

Is the road to Sarah's mountain cabin a bad road? What is a "bad road?" A road could be bad because it has steep hills or sharp curves, or because it is narrow or deeply rutted. Each of these characteristics, in turn, requires further specification (how steep is a steep hill?). Many different definitions are possible, and each one could, with care, be worded so as to pass the clairvoyance test. Which definition should we use? To choose the best definition, we need to know why the question was asked. What decision rests on the answer? If the question was asked because the county is considering taking over the road, the best definition of "bad road" may be "costs more than $2000 to bring up to county standards." But if the decision is whether you will visit the cabin this weekend, the best definition of "bad road" may be something like "Cannot be negotiated by a 1980 VW Rabbit in second gear without damage to the car."

Exercises for Section 2.3

1. The second question in the exercises for Section 2.2 asked you to rewrite a horoscope. Do all the components of the rewritten horoscope pass the clairvoyance test? If not, improve them.
2. Define the following phrases so that they will pass the clairvoyance test. Give two definitions for each phrase.

   a. A clever man
   b. A thrilling book
   c. A frightening movie
   d. A grave situation
   e. A just trial
   f. A good teacher
   g. Nice weather
   h. A wealthy man

3. The definitions you gave in question 2 were probably narrower than the ordinary meaning of the phrases. For each phrase, give an example that suits the ordinary meaning of it, but does not fall under either of your two definitions.

3 Listing and Grouping Possible Answers

3.1 THE IMPORTANCE OF CONSIDERING ALL POSSIBLE ANSWERS

In a day care center, the teacher was shocked to realize that a three-year-old child was missing. She had arrived at the day care center as usual, played with other kids, had a snack with them, and an hour after snack was found to be missing. The teacher asked the neighbors to help him look for the child in the area surrounding the day care building: "She probably did not go far away in one hour; she's only three years old." When the search was in vain the teacher called the police. Police forces got organized for the searching process. They listed the possible whereabouts of the missing child:

1. Inside the day care ("Perhaps she wanted to hide somewhere and fell asleep.").
2. In the area surrounding the day care, within a radius of half a mile ("A three-year-old child is not capable of going very far in an hour's time.").
3. In a park two miles from the day care ("Perhaps she was taken there by somebody.").
4. In any other place, farther than half a mile away ("Perhaps she climbed in a parked car that began moving.").

Only after raising those alternatives did the police forces begin their search.

If we compare the way the police forces responded to the situation to the way the teacher did, we can see the police were much more efficient. The teacher didn't think about different possibilities concerning the whereabouts of the child. He centered his actions around the one possibility that he thought was most likely. The police also raised the possibility that the child was somewhere near the day care center, but they considered other possibilities as well. The child may finally be found near the day care center, proving that the teacher was right, but we have previously learned not to judge a decision process according to its result. The fact that the child was actually found to be in the neighborhood does not prove that the thought processes of eliciting and acting on only one possibility is the right process.

When we think about a problem toward which we feel uncertain, there are some advantages in listing all the possible answers, even the less likely ones:

1. The elicitation of other possibilities, with reasons for them, weakens our overconfidence in the first elicited possibility. If the teacher had spoken with the police, listening to their possibilities and arguments, probably his confidence in the idea that the child is near the building would have been weakened. He would probably have thought, "I have to admit that I didn't think about those possibilities."

2. When one raises only one possibility, activities directed at other possibilities are completely neglected. All efforts are centered around one most favorite possibility—all the neighbors looked for the child around the day care center. Even if, after considering all possibilities, action were to be focused on just one possibility, the explicit listing of the other possibilities prepares us mentally for those other possibilities. If the child is finally found in the park, it will be easier to adjust to the idea that she is there much more quickly than if we had not thought about it before. We will be less surprised to find out that she is in the park after raising this as a possible place than if we had never thought about it at all.

3. The listing of other possibilities can also be of practical importance. If the child is not found near the day care center, searchers will be more quickly sent to other places. There are also situations in which it will be possible and efficient to act on many possibilities simultaneously, sending some searchers nearby and some to the park.

4. One does not always act in accordance with the most probable possibility. Even if the police believe that it is most probable that the child is near the day care center, they may prefer sending searchers to the park, where there is a deep pool, because it is much more dangerous for the child. In those situations, it is most important to think in advance about many possibilities, even those that are unlikely.

> It is not appropriate to focus on the first possible solution
> that comes to mind concerning a problem. It is better to
> think, in advance, about all possibilities.

This process of listing all possibilities in advance enables us to choose a possibility that is judged by us to be the most suitable (not necessarily always the most probable). Moreover, we can prepare ourselves mentally and practically for additional possibilities judged by us to be less probable. Finally, listing all possibilities enables us to plan for simultaneous action relevant to several possibilities. For example, the designers of nuclear power plants try to think of all possible ways the plant could fail so that they can design safety systems for all those possibilities.

How should we list all possibilities? How should we organize them? There are better and worse ways to do it. These topics are discussed in the next section.

Exercises for Section 3.1

1. List as many possibilities as you can to explain the following situation: ". . . he woke up and looked at his watch; the small hand pointed to five. Some light entered the room. His wife was not near him. He remembered that she told him she would come home at midnight. He became anxious. He ran to his phone and called his parents. His father answered in a drowsy voice. No, his wife is not here. He asked whether perhaps his wife arrived while his father was sleeping. He got a negative answer. He considered his next steps."

2. My car won't start. List the ten most likely causes.

3. The phone rang at six a.m. When you answered it, there was only a dial tone. Why? List the five most likely possibilities.

3.2 STRUCTURING POSSIBILITY LISTS

Example A: You meet a person. Was this person born in Canada? The problem is clearly defined, and it is easy to list the possibilities. There are only two: (1) Yes; (2) No.

Example B: I have a die in my hand. On which side will it fall? The possibilities are: (1) one (2) two (3) three (4) four (5) five (6) six.

Example C: I have a current American coin in my hand. Which coin is it? The list is:

(1) penny
(2) nickel
(3) dime
(4) quarter
(5) half-dollar
(6) dollar

We will call such lists "lists of possibilities." In all three examples, it is easy to list all possibilities. But if the question in Example A had been "In what country was this person born?" many possibilities would come to mind. All the countries in the world are possible. In a situation where there are many possibilities, we often will not want to, or not be able to, list all the possibilities.

> When we have many possibilities, it is worthwhile to group them into categories; each category will contain a number of possibilities.

Grouping into categories is guided by a certain *rule*. For example, we could group the countries according to continents. Thus, there are six categories of possibilities (one for each of the six continents); each category (continent) will contain a number of possibilities (countries). The categorization could be guided by a different rule, for example, language. English speaking countries, French speaking countries, and so on. The number of categories will be the number of languages.[1]

Categorization is not a process that we use only in uncertain situations. We encounter such a process daily under another name: *classification*. Example: A library is interested in organizing a catalogue of books so that people can easily find a specific book they need. The books have to be classified according to one or more specific rules. A book can be classified according to one of the following systems or according to several of them simultaneously.

1. Classification according to *subject*. Each subject (topic) will be a category and in each category the number of possibilities will be the number of books on this subject.

---

[1] There are a few countries with more than one official language. These will cause problems for grouping, which we will discuss later.

2. Alphabetical classification according to the *title* of the book—each letter is a category and the number of possibilities in each category is the number of books whose title begins with that letter.

3. Alphabetical classification according to *name of author*. Again, each letter of the alphabet is a category. Any other classification is possible as long as it is useful.

One can subdivide any list of possibilities (see Fig. 3.1a) into few wide categories each of which contains many possibilities (see Fig. 3.1b) or into many narrow categories each of which contains few possibilities (see Fig. 3.1c); an extreme case is the case in which each possibility has a different category (see again Fig. 3.1a).

The decision concerning the number of categories depends, of course, on the problem, on the purpose of the classification. When one has to rely on one's memory, about 5 to 7 categories are most efficient. More than 7 categories places a strain on our cognitive abilities, whereas fewer than 5 may leave too many possibilities in each category.

Let us look at another classification problem: How should you file the bills on your desk? You want a system that is logical, so that you can quickly find an old bill when you need it. You could file them by month: all bills paid in one month go in the same file. Alternatively, you could file them by payee: all the phone bills go in one file. Can you think of any other efficient filing system?

Exercises for Section 3.2

1. Group the possibilities you raised in questions 1 and 2 of Section 3.1 into categories. Give a name to each category.
2. Classify the books in your private library into five to seven categories. Give a name to each category. What is your classification rule?

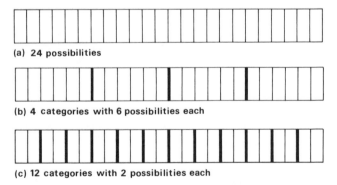

(a) **24 possibilities**

(b) **4 categories with 6 possibilities each**

(c) **12 categories with 2 possibilities each**

FIG. 3.1   Categorization of 24 possibilities.

3.3 NECESSARY REQUIREMENTS FOR CATEGORY LISTS

Clear definition. Just as a problem has to be clearly defined and pass the clairvoyance test, so do all the categories (or the possibilities, if we don't group). We have to define the category names so that the clairvoyant could say without any doubt in which category every possibility falls. If the police forces asked the clairvoyant, "Where is the child? In the day care center, around it, or far from it?" the clairvoyant wouldn't have been able to answer because it isn't clear what exactly is meant by "around the day care center" or "far." But if asked "Where is the child—in the day care, near it within a radius of half a mile, or more than a half a mile away?", the clairvoyant could have answered.

Another example:

Alice: How many burglaries were committed in your neighborhood last year?

Tony: Not so many.

Maybe Alice knows what Tony means by "not so many," but the clairvoyant does not. The clairvoyant could not answer the question, "How many burglaries were there—few, not so many, or many?" The clairvoyant knows that there were exactly 10 burglaries, but is 10 few, not so many, or many? The clairvoyant *can* answer the question, "How many burglaries were there? (a) less than 10; (b) 10 or more but less than 50; (c) 50 or more."

It is not always easy to give precise definitions to all categories. Often the differences are not very clear and the boundaries between categories are vague. For example, when you get a driver's license, you must state your eye color. Eye colors are problematic in the sense that they are not clearly defined. When does blue become green? In spite of those difficulties, the usual classification is: (1) black (2) brown or hazel (3) grey (4) blue (5) green. However, even the clairvoyant may have difficulty in deciding how to categorize the eyes of someone whose eyes are bluish green, varying with the color of clothing. The categories are not well defined. (One could define eye color on the basis of wave lengths, but the measurement would be expensive and not very practical.) In difficult cases like that we should agree, in advance, on a *classification method* for assigning each possibility to a category. One method is to specify, in advance, that there is a *judge* who decides how to classify each case. For a driver's license, the applicant is the judge; all people decide what their own eye color is. In other situations, we can select a judge, or even require that two people agree on the classification, with a third person to resolve ties. We could, for example, specify an expert who will decide, for countries in which more than one language is spoken, what the primary language is.

As we call for strictness in the clear definition of the problem, so we will have to be very strict about a clear definition of the categories. It is important so that each possibility has a place in the classification, and there will be no arguments. When clear definitions are difficult, we will overcome the difficulty by specifying a classification method in advance.

Sometimes developing clear definitions for categories will serve to clarify a vague problem. For example, we could develop categories by which to classify roads. The category "bad road" might be roads that have potholes or ruts more than 4 inches deep, and so forth. Such category definitions would then clarify what is meant by the question, "Is the road bad?"

Clear definition is a necessary condition for a good list of categories, but it is not a sufficient condition. For a good list we will need further requirements.

Exhaustiveness. Each list of categories must be exhaustive, that is, it must be capable of including all possibilities.

In the classification of motor vehicles, the license bureau creates categories such that all motor vehicles will have a place: trucks, buses, taxis, private cars, motorcycles, and special cars.

When we say that the year is divided into four seasons, autumn, winter, spring, and summer, each of the 12 months can be assigned to a season.

It is not always easy to create an exhaustive list.

Example A. I decided to classify the books in my private library according to subject. I could put most of my books under one of these categories: (1) fiction (2) poetry (3) science (4) philosophy (5) art. After putting most of the books into these categories, I find some books left: A dictionary, a book of puzzles, three cookbooks, and a book on photography. I could add more categories, one category for each of those books, but then I would have too many categories, some of them with one item only.

A more practical solution for the above problems would be to add only one additional category to which all the remaining books will belong. The name of this category could be "other" or "miscellaneous." The additional category will assure that the list will be exhaustive—every book in my library can be categorized. For the classification of motor vehicles mentioned above, "special cars" was actually the miscellaneous category.

Example B. The editor of the local newspaper grouped the news into four categories: (1) international news (2) national news (3) local news (4) economic news. News for these four categories comes across the desk every day, but what about all other news? A new Miss Universe was elected, a new research on cancer has promising results, and so on. Should the editor add more categories for medical news, for beauty competitions, or for anything else that comes along? This would be ridiculous; almost every day some unpredictable events happen that wouldn't fit into any category. Again, it is worthwhile adding only one more category, "miscellaneous," into which all the other news will be grouped. In this way, we ensure that the list of categories is exhaustive, there are not too many categories, and there is a proper place for unusual or unpredictable news. Go back to the example at the start of this chapter; you will see that the list of categories the police developed concerning the whereabouts of the child was actually an exhaustive list.

A miscellaneous category is especially important in uncertain situations, when it is difficult to think about all possibilities in advance.

Exclusiveness. We now add a further requirement. Not only should every case have a place, but it should have *one and only one place.* The categories have to be defined in such a way that not more than one of them will include the same possibility. Ruth and Nancy have a game: a board with squares on it, dice and toy soldiers. They decided to invent new rules for the game so that it will be more interesting. Each player tries to move her soldiers to the opposite side. The one who moves all her soldiers first will win. The rules for moving are as follows:

Each player in turn throws the dice.
1. If she gets an even number, she will progress as many squares as shown on the dice.
2. If she gets an odd number, she will retreat as many squares as shown on the dice.
3. If she gets a number divisible by 3, she does not move.

The two kids begin playing. Ruth throws the dice and gets a 6. "Marvelous, I can progress six steps." "No," responds Nancy, "Six is divisible by 3, you have to stay where you are."

Of course, Ruth and Nancy's new rules are no good because one outcome was represented by two rules (possibilities); six is an even number and a number divisible by 3. In other words, the categories were not *exclusive.* In the above example, poor grouping caused only an argument, but if the police forces search all possible areas for the missing child, non-exclusive possibilities may cause duplication of effort.

Thus, the third requirement for every list of categories is that the categories in the list of categories must be exclusive. The only way to check whether the categories are exclusive is by logical testing: we have to imagine a case suitable to two or more categories. Consider the following example: In an attempt to create categories for vertebrates, we decided on five categories: (1) mammals (2) reptiles (3) birds (4) creatures with fins (5) other. Is there a vertebrate that is included in more than one category? Yes, the whale is a mammal and has fins; thus, it belongs in both the first and the fourth category. The categories are therefore nonexclusive. In the same way, we could think about the piece of news that is simultaneously "national news" and "economic news." Often it is easy to overcome nonexclusiveness by redefining the categories. Try the biological division of vertebrates: fish, amphibians, reptiles, birds, and mammals.

Sometimes it is difficult to create exclusive categories, as with the news problem. One of the following solutions can be adopted:

a. Allow the person who groups the items the freedom to decide in which category to put the possibility. (This solution is like the solution we proposed when the categories didn't have clear definitions.) The news editor will decide how to classify each piece of news.

b. Use "miscellaneous" as a category for all ambivalent cases. Then, each category will be defined as: "predominantly economic news," "predominantly international news," and so forth. The miscellaneous category will include, for example, news about an international economic problem. The disadvantage of such a solution is that the miscellaneous category quickly becomes too big a category. Try to avoid using these two solutions whenever possible. Instead, try to find a list of naturally exclusive categories.

Let us summarize all three requirements for making lists of possibilities in uncertain situations:

---

1. Each category of possibilities must be clearly defined.
2. The list of categories must be exhaustive—include all expected and unexpected cases.
3. The list of categories must be exclusive—each possibility should fit into only one category.

In a sense, these three requirements can always be met by technical means. One can achieve clear definitions by specifying a judge; then each category is defined in terms of that judge's decisions. Exhaustiveness can always be achieved by adding one more category, "other." Exclusiveness can be achieved artificially by limiting each category to possibilities that cannot belong in any other category, and saving the "other" or "miscellaneous" category for all mixed possibilities, thus:

A. All A's that are not also B's or C's.
B. All B's that are not also A's or C's.

C. All C's that are not also A's or B's.

D. All other.

However, such technical solutions do not always lead to the most useful categorizations. Additional characteristics of useful categories are discussed in the next section.

Exercises for Section 3.3

1. In question 2 of Section 3.2, you classified the books in your library. Check that the list of categories you created satisfies the above three requirements.

2. Check and criticize the following lists of possibilities:

    a. What will the color of the traffic light be when I arrive at the intersection?

       1. red

       2. yellow

       3. green

    b. How will the coin fall?

       1. heads

       2. tails

    c. How many coins are in my pocket?

       1. 0–4

       2. 4–6

       3. 6–8

       4. 8–10

    d. What is his profession?

       1. scientist

       2. writer

       3. blue collar

       4. teacher

       5. other

    e. What book are you reading?

       1. prose

       2. poetry

       3. scientific literature

       4. professional literature

    f. Where did the tourist come from?

       1. Japan

       2. Europe

       3. Australia

       4. New York

3. For each of the lists you criticized in question 2, suggest a better list. If you have difficulties, list them.

3.4   MORE REQUIREMENTS FOR LISTS OF CATEGORIES

Each list of categories must pass some necessary requirements. But for many problems, we can create more than one list of categories, all of which satisfy those requirements. Which one of these well-defined, exhaustive, and exclusive lists is most efficient? Let's go back to the missing child example. We have to devise a search plan for her. One possible list of categories is the following:

1. Inside the day care center.
2. Within a radius of less than 100 yards of the day care center.
3. Within a radius of 100 yards or more but less than 500 yards from the day care center.
4. Within a radius of 500 yards or more but less than a mile from around the day care center.
5. Within a radius of one mile or more but less than five miles from the day care center.
6. All other possibilities.

This list passes all three requirements: The categories are well defined, exhaustive, and exclusive. But we can suggest another list of categories for the same problem: (1) the child is with a relative; (2) the child is with friends of the family; (3) the child is with strangers; and (4) other possibilities. This list is also well defined, exhaustive, and exclusive. Those two lists stress a different *aspect* of the same problem. The first list is focused on distance from the day care center. The second list focuses on the question "Whom is the child with?" The decision about which list to use depends primarily on the purpose of the listing. In this example, it depends on how the police chief wants to organize the search. Should the forces be sent to search in areas around the day care center, or is it more efficient to send them to look for family members and friends? If the police chief believes that the child is not just wandering around somewhere but is with someone, one of her friends or relatives, the chief would probably prefer the second list of possibilities.

Consider another classification problem. The area of a certain city can be divided into sub-areas in different ways according to different purposes (see Fig. 3.2). There is a division of the city into neighborhoods; this is a division which is important for city management in order to provide services to all

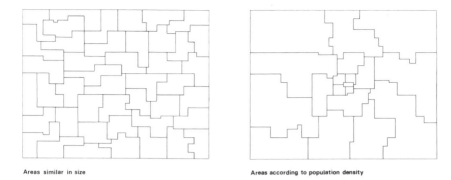

Areas similar in size   Areas according to population density

FIG. 3.2   Dividing a city into sub-areas.

neighborhoods. The same city can be divided according to the density of
population so that the mail can be delivered efficiently. In the first division,
according to neighborhoods, each sub-area is approximately the same size.
In the second division, the sub-areas vary greatly in size.

> The selection of a set of categories depends on the purpose of
> the categorization.

Often, the important aspects of the problem emerge from the definition
of the problem itself; we are then not free to choose the categories. The title
of a local radio news show is "News Across the Country." In this case, the
grouping of the news is according to areas and not subjects. Similarly, in the
case of the missing child, if we ask "Whom did the child leave with?" the
question directs us to a specific list of possibilities.

In other cases, the categories are given, and we learn about specific
aspects of the problem from the categories. Suppose the problem is "How
do Americans spend their free time?" Consider two lists:
List A:

1. Entertainment inside the house (TV, conversation, etc.).
2. Indoor entertainment not in one's house (concerts, theater, etc.).
3. Outdoor entertainment (trips, sports, etc.).
4. Miscellaneous.

List B:

1. Solitary entertainment (reading, TV, etc.).
2. Active social entertainment (dancing, conversation, etc.).

3. Passive social entertainment (movies, lectures, etc.).

4. Miscellaneous.

Each of these lists presents one aspect of the problem: List A stresses the *place* of entertainment; List B stresses the amount of *social interaction.* One can think about a third list that stresses the amount of time spent. The purpose of the listing is revealed by the categories. In this situation, even if the problem is not well defined, one can learn about the purpose of listing from the names of the categories.

After we chose a specific aspect of a problem (searching according to "distance" vs. "people"), we can still group the possibilities into categories in different ways. List A: with relatives, with friends, with strangers, miscellaneous. List B: with her sister, with her uncle, with Michael, miscellaneous. Again, the preference for one of these lists over the other depends on the purpose of the classification. For the police it may be more important to know the exact names of people than to work with general categories.

> Even if the aspect is known, selection of a list of categories depends on the purpose of the categorization.

There is one more point worth mentioning. When there are so many possibilities that we want to group them into categories and when there are no special requirements leading us to group according to specific aspects, it is desirable to have approximately the same number of possibilities in each category. An invitation to a potluck often specifies "If your name begins with one of the letters A through D, bring a salad. E through K, bring a main dish. L through Q, dessert. R through Z, drinks." These categories were selected by counting the pages in a telephone directory, to ensure that approximately 25% of all names fall in each category. When such a system is used the potluck should have approximately the same number of salads as main dishes, and so on.

In problems involving uncertainty, this idea expresses itself as a requirement that we will try to group possibilities in such a way that each category is more or less equally likely. If telephone employees are assigned to answer questions and complaints, an assignment based on single letters of the alphabet wouldn't equally distribute the work load. The employee answering only the complaints from people whose last name starts with "I" would have little to do, while the "S" person would be swamped. But if the alphabet were categorized as it was for the potluck, the probability of a caller having a last name that falls in a given category is approximately the same for all four categories. Assigning employees on this basis would thus equalize the work load.

To summarize: categories for the possibilities of an uncertain situation must be clearly defined, exhaustive, and exclusive. When these criteria are met, categories should be chosen to reflect the central aspects of the problem. Finally, whenever possible it is efficient to select categories in such a way that all are approximately equally likely.

Exercises for Section 3.4

1. For each of the following problems, prepare a good and efficient list of categories.

    A. John came home from work and found no one at home. Why?
    B. My sister is ill. What is her illness?
    C. What is the height of the tallest man to pass by your window within the next hour?
    D. The fire began in the factory. What caused it?
    E. What kind of sandwich is that?
    F. What kind of car will your friend buy?
    G. My Time Magazine didn't arrive. Why?

2. Two people are interested in each of the following problems. For each problem, create a list of possibilities for each person.

    A. What score will I get in the biology exam?
        1st interested person: a good student
        2nd interested person: a bad student
    B. What will the weather be like tomorrow?
        1st interested person: a soldier with a long march tomorrow
        2nd interested person: an organizer of a competition for model airplanes
    C. I called Allan and there was no answer. Why?
        1st interested person: his friend
        2nd interested person: a thief
    D. What flower do I hold in my hand?
        1st interested person: a botany expert
        2nd interested person: a child
    E. How much does this cake cost?
        1st interested person: a person who is going to buy it
        2nd interested person: a person who has only one dollar
    F. A truck was stuck in the middle of the intersection and couldn't get started. What is the reason?
        1st interested person: the driver of the truck
        2nd interested person: a police officer

4 Defining Degrees of Belief

4.1 INTRODUCTION

The elicitation of a good set of possibilities is a necessary step for taking reasonable actions or making decisions. However, it is not a sufficient step. Even when the set of possibilities is well defined, exhaustive, and exclusive, the listing of possibilities does not, in itself, indicate which decision or action is best. For the decision as to how to deploy the police searching for the missing child (see Chapter 3), the listing of the possible whereabouts of the child is not enough. The decision depends on our confidence in each one of the possibilities (as well as on other considerations). Thus, an additional necessary step in any decision we make is to define our confidence or degree of belief in any one of the elicited possibilities. In Chapter 1 we saw that the degree of belief is a personal, subjective feeling; its external manifestation can give an outsider an idea about it. In the present chapter, we will inquire into the ways we usually express degree of belief, and we will discuss how it actually *should be done.*

4.2 USUAL EXPRESSIONS OF CONFIDENCE

Consider these expressions of degrees of belief:

a. Jones: Will we win the case?
   The lawyer: *There is a chance* we will.

b. Smith: If I buy a new $200 part for my car, will it bring an end to the car's frequent needed repairs?

The mechanic: I can't guarantee that, but the *chances are not negligible.*

c. Carol: David, are you coming to the concert tonight?

David: *Maybe.*

d. Physicians: Ms. Miller, I recommend that you undergo an operation which is not easy and even risky, but it is worth doing.

Ms. Miller: What are the chances that the operation will succeed?

Physician: There's a *good chance.*

e. Ben (to the palm reader): Will I pass the examination?

Palm reader: It's *very likely.*

f. Paul: Do you think it will rain tomorrow?

Bill: *Probably*; it is cloudy outside.

Don: Do you think it will snow?

Bill: That's *probable,* too.

Mark: But *less probable* than rain.

These six examples are concerned with uncertain situations. The mechanic, physician, and even the palm reader can't give a certain answer to the questions they are asked. Each one of them chose one answer and indicated their degree of belief in it. This degree of belief is expressed in different ways using different verbal expressions: "there is a chance," "maybe," "very likely," and "probably." In daily conversations and in the news media we often hear verbal expressions that convey the speaker's degree of belief in one or more possibilities. Do those words clearly express the speaker's degree of belief? Does the listener get a clear picture of the speaker's subjective feelings? Ms. Miller was told that her operation has a "good chance" of success. What does this mean? The mechanic claimed that "the chances are not negligible"; what did he really mean by that?

In Chapter 2 we discussed the ambiguity of our daily language. There we were concerned with ambiguity in the definition of uncertain situations. We recommended that the question or situation be defined clearly to avoid misunderstandings and wrong decisions. Just as there is much ambiguity in the definition of uncertain situations, there is also much ambiguity in the expressions indicating degree of belief, as can be seen in the above examples. In daily usage of language, the *same* person often uses *different* words to express the *same* amount of belief. Moreover, the *same* word is used by the *same* person to express *different* degrees of belief (see example f).

This vagueness and ambiguity prevents comparisons among different expressions of degrees of belief. It is difficult to rank the words to determine which one expresses a higher degree of belief. Try ranking the following words according to the amount of degrees of belief they express, from the smallest to the highest:

    a good chance
    quite likely
    a fighting chance
    probable
    rather likely
    maybe

It is difficult, sometimes impossible, to build a scale out of such words. Is "probable" more likely than "rather likely?" What is the meaning of "maybe" and "a fighting chance?" Where exactly is their place in the scale? Even if you can build a scale of words expressing degree of belief, a comparison between your scale and the scales of others will show how much disagreement there is.

Furthermore, if we arrive at an agreed scale, we will not be able to define exactly the relationships between the scale steps. How *much* more likely is "quite likely" than "rather likely?" What is half as probable as "a good chance?" Such vague expressions for degrees of belief cause much misunderstanding. The speaker and the listener often don't share the same meanings. A long debate can result from such ambiguities.

One can claim that although the language is full of ambiguous expressions, we generally understand one another quite well; moreover, it is not always so important to be precise and clear. Sometimes, indeed, it would be ridiculous to require such clarity. Although this is often the case, it is not a justification for ambiguity in other situations. Carol in Example C may be satisfied with David's answer about his possible presence at the concert, if his presence or absence is not going to affect her decision to go. But if his presence is going to affect her decision, his answer may be too vague. She doesn't expect him to answer with certainty (since he himself is uncertain), but wants to know *how* uncertain he is. Are the chances high, low, or very low? His answer conveys only uncertainty, and fails to indicate his strength or degree of belief.

When making decisions in uncertain situations, the ambiguity of verbal expressions intended to convey degree of belief makes a decision more difficult. The lawyer's, mechanic's, and physician's answers don't help their clients much. Does the lawyer's answer, "there is a chance," mean that the chance is high enough to justify the money and time that will be spent in the judicial process? Do the mechanic's "not negligible" chances justify spending $200?

> Vague expressions of degree or belief can:
> a. cause misunderstandings
> b. complicate the decision process and lead to unwise decisions.

In daily conversation, there are ways to overcome ambiguity in verbal expressions of degree of belief; we use hand gestures, facial expressions, and often vocal inflections. One can express the sentence, "there is a chance" differently using different vocal inflection that will indicate either a small chance or a large chance (try it). But in written language these devices will not help.

Another way to overcome ambiguity is to create a common scale of words in a group of people who are engaged in a decision process. This will be, of course, an arbitrary scale, suitable for, and agreed to, by the specific group. This solution may be good for some cases, but it doesn't solve all the problems. An intelligence officer gets hourly information concerning the enemy's troop movements. On the basis of this information, she is asked to express her daily degree of belief in an outbreak of war. The changes in her feelings from one day to another may be very small, but those small changes may strongly affect a decision to mobilize the reserve forces. Even an agreed-upon scale of verbal expressions may not be sufficient to distinguish small but important differences in degrees of belief.

Another disadvantage of verbal expressions of degrees of belief is demonstrated in the following two examples:

The chances of war are equal to the chances of rolling a six with a fair die.

Mr. Baker has a minor medical problem, the presence of which affects his daily life only slightly. The problem can be solved with a complicated operation. The chances for its success (removing the problem) are equal to the chances of rolling a six with a fair die.

Although the chances expressed in both examples are identical (both are identical to the chances of rolling a six), people don't judge it this way. The chances of war will verbally be expressed as "high" or "considerable," whereas the chances of the success of the operation will be expressed as "small" or "negligible." Why? In the judgment of degrees of belief, chances, probabilities, and so on, we tend to take into consideration values, gains, and losses. The chance of war breaking out is called "considerable" because of the high losses involved in it. The same chance, in Mr. Baker's case, is judged as "low" since one can live a decent life with the problem and because the operation's risks are high.

For decision making under uncertainty (shall we call up reserves?) one has to take account of each possibility's chances (will they attack or not?) and the values, gains, and losses associated with each possibility. It is important to convey to the decision maker a *separate* picture concerning the chances (degrees of belief) and the values. If Ms. Miller (in Example D) wants to make a decision concerning the operation, the physician should give her a *separate* evaluation of the chances of success and the pain, cost, and so forth. By saying "good chance," the physician implicitly conveys his advice concerning whether or not the operation should be performed, but does not clearly express his belief concerning whether the operation would be a success.

For good communication between people and for good decision making processes, it is important that the expression indicating degree of belief indicates strength of belief only, and not an evaluation of that strength in the context of the decision problem. Such an evaluation can be expressed in a second stage after the strength of belief has been clearly expressed. The verbal expressions for degree of belief tend to confuse those two aspects of an evaluation.

Four disadvantages of using verbal expressions to express degrees of belief are:

1. The usage and understanding of such expressions are inconsistent both within a person over different occasions and between people on the same occasion.

2. Any one of these expressions conveys varying degrees of belief depending on the context.

3. These expressions are not sufficiently sensitive to small but important changes in degrees of belief.

4. These expressions may confuse strength of belief with expressions of value.

In the light of these disadvantages, we seek a different tool to express our degrees of belief that will be understood unambiguously by everybody, will enable us to make comparisons between different degrees of belief, will be sensitive to small changes in degrees of belief, and will distinguish between the quantitative dimension (strength of belief) and the evaluative dimension (values, gains, and losses).

Exercises for Section 4.2

1. Find in the newspaper at least 5 paragraphs in which there is a verbal expression of degree of belief.

2. A horoscope is a way to deal with uncertainty. Choose one horoscope and point out words which express degree of belief.

3. Rank the expressions you collected in Exercises 1 and 2 from the expression that indicates the smallest degree of belief to the one that indicates the highest. What are the difficulties you encounter?

4.3 NUMERICAL EXPRESSIONS OF CONFIDENCE

What are the chances that the Boston Red Sox will win the American League pennant next year?

John: 50–50, because the New York Yankees might win it, too.
Don: 100%.

John and Don express their degrees of belief in the possibility that "the Boston Red Sox will win the American League pennant next year." They don't express it in words, but in numbers: 50 and 100. We understand exactly their feelings: Don is much more confident than John. We will adopt their way of expressing degrees of belief.

Let us assume that each one of us has a full store of confidence. When you feel completely confident about something, when you feel certainty, you will express it by saying that you attribute your whole store of confidence to it, 100% of it. I am completely confident that I am reading now; I feel certainty regarding it. I give 100% of my confidence to it. On the other hand, when we feel uncertainty regarding a question, our store of confidence is distributed among the possible answers according to our degree of belief in each. John believes that it is just as likely that the Boston Red Sox will win or not win the pennant. He therefore divided 100% confidence evenly between the two possibilities: the Boston Red Sox *will* win the American League pennant and the Boston Red Sox *will not* win the American League pennant. Oliver may think that the chances of the Boston Red Sox are much higher than those of the other teams; he gives 70% of his confidence to the possibility that the Boston team will win, and only 30% of his confidence to the possibility that Boston will not win. John, Oliver, and Don divide their store of confidence differently between the two possibilities.

Let us describe the total store of confidence with a circle of a constant area. The division of our store of confidence to all the possibilities is shown in Fig. 4.1 with pie-shaped sectors of the circle. Don, John, and Oliver's answers can be described in the following way:

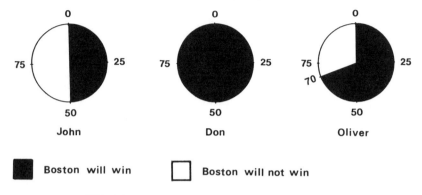

FIG. 4.1   Different divisions of stores of confidence.

The division of confidence may be different from person to person, since degrees of belief are personal, subjective feelings. However, there is something common to all numbers: the numbers assigned to all the possibilities add up to 100. If the confidence store is 100%, and if we divide it among exclusive and exhaustive possibilities, then we have to use it all up. The two possibilities that the Boston Red Sox will win or that they will not win are, of course, exclusive and exhaustive possibilities, since no tie is possible. When one has two such possibilities, one can infer, of course, from the chances given to one possibility about the chances given to the other one.

> The number we assign to a possibility expresses the percentage of our store of confidence.

If the list of possibilities we elicited is exhaustive and if the possibilities are mutually exclusive, then the sum of the degrees of belief given to each possibility must add up to 100%. If, after the distribution of numbers to all possibilities, we realize that they sum up to less than 100%, then either: (a) we attributed too little of our confidence to one of the possibilities; or (b) the list of possibilities is not exhaustive. If the numbers sum up to more than 100, then either: (a) we attributed too much confidence to one of the possibilities; or (b) the possibilities are not exclusive.

The following example is adapted from Chapter 1: "What is the longest river in the world?" (1) the Nile (2) the Mississippi (3) the Amazon (4) other. Ray and Ben were not sure regarding any one of the possible answers. They divided their stores of confidence differently.

	Ray			*Ben*	
1.	Mississippi	30	1.	Mississippi	50
2.	Nile	35	2.	Nile	30
3.	Amazon	20	3.	Amazon	10
4.	Other	15	4.	Other	10
		100			100

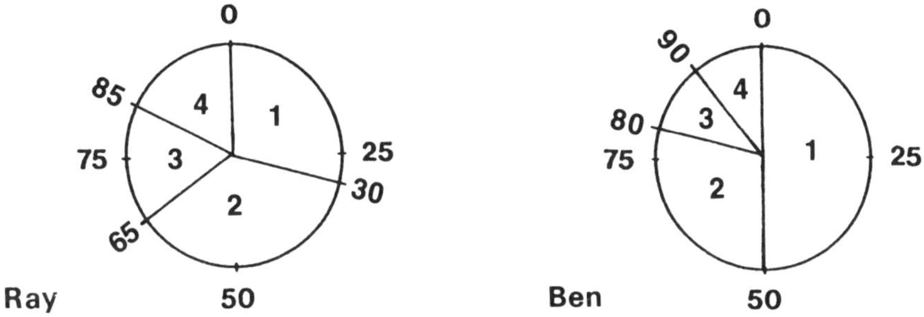

FIG. 4.2   More divisions of stores of confidence.

In Fig. 4.2 we see that Ray feels more uncertainty than Ben; Ray distributed his confidence more evenly between the four possibilities.

Exercises for Section 4.3

1. Consider the verbal expressions you collected for question 1 of the last section.
   a. If you had to translate each phrase into a number indicating percentage of confidence, what number would you choose?
   b. You probably are not completely sure about your numerical translation. Give an upper and lower limit to your translation such that you will be nearly certain that the word indicates a percentage in the given interval.
   c. Rank the words according to the *range* of the interval. Can you learn something about the words from the range of the intervals?

2. Following are a number of possibility lists with numerical degrees of belief assigned to each. But the numbers don't add up to 100. For each list, decide whether the list is wrong (the possibilities are not exhaustive and/or not exclusive) or the fault is with the distribution of probabilities. Then correct the problem you found.

   a. When will they install a new telephone in our house?
      today—10
      within 3 days—40

within a week—80
within two weeks—95
other—5

b. What kind of car will stop to pick up those two hitchhikers?
private car or truck—60
commercial truck—25
tow truck—5
taxi—20
bus—5
other—10

c. Where did I first meet him?
in high school—20
at college—25
at a party—15
in my neighborhood—10
at a football game—20

d. Why didn't Henry call me as he promised?
he forgot—30
he intentionally didn't call—5
the telephone was out of order—10
the telephone was busy—2
other—30

e. Why won't the car start?
electrical problems—30
dead battery—50
out of gas—30
engine flooded—20
other—25

4.4 THE ADVANTAGES OF NUMERICAL EXPRESSIONS

When Ray and Ben distributed their confidence among the four possibilities, we immediately knew who is more certain and who is less, who is more confident in his chosen answer and who is less. The numerical language as an expression of degrees of belief has a number of advantages over verbal language.

Numbers overcome the ambiguity and vagueness of verbal expressions. They are interpreted identically by all users. The number expresses a percentage of all confidence attributed to an answer or an event. When John says 50% to the chances that the Boston Red Sox will win the American League Pennant, we know exactly how he feels. He means, and we understand, all of these things:

50% of his store of confidence is attributed to the possibility that they will win.

50% of his confidence is attributed to the possibility that they will not win.

The chances that they will win and the chances that they will not win are perceived by him to be identical.

We understand that John's degrees of belief can be diagrammed thusly: ——————————➤

John has the same degree of belief in the Red Sox's winning as he does in a fair coin ending up heads.

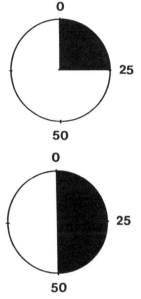

When a politician says that the chances that a peace treaty between Israel and the Arab countries will be signed before the end of the year 2000 are 25%, he means (and we understand) that his confidence divides thusly: ——————➤

As can be seen, the same number always expresses the same degree of belief. Different degrees of belief are expressed by different numbers. Every number has one meaning, identical for the speaker and the listener.

There is no controversy concerning the relative strength of different numbers. Fifteen percent is higher than 7% and lower than 32%. If two possibilities are assigned 75% and 25%, then the chances given to the first are three times as great as those given to the second. Thus, numbers enable us to make precise comparisons among different degrees of belief.

With numbers, we can express small differences in degrees of belief. Suppose that the intelligence officer who receives information about the enemy's troop movements uses numbers to express, each day, her degree of belief in the outbreak of war. Such numbers may be used in conjunction with a decision rule. For example, the rule may specify that if the chances are above 10%, part of the reserves are called up; if they are above 20%, more of the reserves are called up, and so on. The differences between 10% and 20% may not be clearly conveyed and perceived with verbal expressions. Often, as in this example, a decision maker has a threshold on the chance scale beneath which one action is taken and above which another action is taken. Such threshold points can be a result of a long decision analysis. A decision maker using such threshold points needs exact numbers.

With numbers it is easier to differentiate between the quantity dimension that reflects the strength of the degree of belief and the evaluation dimension reflecting the values inherent in the decision making context. The number expresses chances only; it does not express values. After using a number to express the chances, one could add some words to express one's evaluation concerning those numbers in the decision making context. For example, "a 20% chance of a surprise attack is too high" means, implicitly, that something has to be done about it. However, if the characteristics of an event tend strongly to influence its probability evaluation, it may also affect the given numbers.

---

1. Numbers are understood identically by all users.
2. Numbers allow comparisons between degrees of belief.
3. Numbers can convey small differences in degrees of belief.
4. Numbers separate the quantitative dimension of chances from the evaluative one.

4.5 WHY DO PEOPLE USE VAGUE LANGUAGE TO CONVEY DEGREES OF BELIEF?

If you are convinced that it is much better to use numbers to convey degrees of belief than to use verbal expressions, you probably wonder why most of us continue to use verbal expressions in daily conversation, in the news, and even in academic manuscripts.

Most people are not aware of the problems created by verbal expressions, and therefore don't seek alternative ways to convey degrees of belief. However, some of those who are conscious of the disadvantages of verbal expression refuse to use numbers. For most of the problems people face they have a general feeling regarding the chances, but they find it difficult to translate these feelings into numbers. A number requires a clear specification of the feeling: Are my feelings best expressed as 20%, 30%, or maybe only 10%?

Not only do we find it difficult to translate a vague feeling into a number, but we may believe, in addition, that using a precise number implies exact reasons. When we say, "it's very likely," we do not feel the need to give a detailed justification for our statement, but we do feel this obligation when we use the precision of numbers. We expect to be asked, "Why 60 instead of 55 or 70? How did you arrive at that number?"

Another sense of responsibility that seems to be psychologically associated with the use of numbers to express degrees of belief is the feeling of being responsible for the result. A mechanic may refuse to say 80% for the chances that the car will work for a year without problems, thinking that if it does have problems, he will be accused of a misstatement.

Can we overcome these difficulties?

The difficulty of eliciting numbers: We will propose a method for elicitation in the next section.

The difficulty of justifying the numbers: Since the numbers reflect subjective degrees of belief, it is sometimes difficult to justify them in detail. And it is true that stating a specific number like "80%" makes you sound more committed than using a verbal phrase like "very likely." The very advantage of clarity (communicating unambiguously with others) results in the disadvantage of apparent precision even when you do not feel that precise. In the next section we offer a way of using numbers to express degrees of belief that avoids the implication of precision by giving a range of numbers instead of a single number.

The fear of being responsible for the results: In the first chapter we talked about good decision processes and desired results. We showed that even a good decision process may sometimes be followed by an undesired outcome, but in the long run good decision processes will more often result in desired outcomes than wrong decision processes will. We also argued that one cannot evaluate *one* decision from its results; one has to look at many decisions. We expect a physician to succeed in most operations for which she gave, say, 80% chance of success, but we should not expect her to succeed in *all* of these operations (or in any particular one of them). If people learn not to evaluate one decision process by its result, they may be less concerned about expressing degrees of belief as numbers. For each separate case, a number should not obligate you any more than a word does.

4.6 ELICITING NUMBERS TO EXPRESS DEGREES OF BELIEF

We may overcome the difficulty in eliciting numbers with the help of a small device called a *chance wheel*. This circular device represents our total store of confidence. Around the circle there are numbers from 0 to 100. The device is actually composed of two interlinked circles, one dark and one light. The user can manipulate the device to change the size of the dark sector from 0% to 100% dark. The numbers around the circle indicate what percentage of the circle is dark. In the middle of the circle there is a pointer that we can spin. If we spin the pointer, the chances that it will land in the dark sector are the same as the proportion of the circle that is dark. When we say we assign "25" to the chances that it will rain tomorrow, we mean that 25% of our store of confidence is assigned to the outcome "rain" and the remaining 75% is assigned to the outcome "no rain." These assignments are the same as the chances that the pointer, when spun, will stop in the dark sector (25% chance) or the light sector (75% chance).

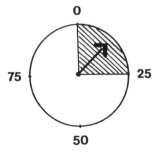

To illustrate the use of a chance wheel, suppose Ellen wishes to elicit from Arthur his degree of belief in the proposition, "In the next election the present mayor of our town will be reelected."

Ellen: What do you think are the chances that in the next election the present mayor will be reelected?

Aruthur: I have no idea.

Ellen: I am sure you have some beliefs about it.

Arthur: Yes, I think that the chances are small.

Ellen: How small?

Arthur: I don't know.

Ellen: Okay, let's find out. I'll offer you two gambles. One gamble involves the mayor. The other involves the chance wheel. In either gamble you can either win $100 or lose nothing. All you have to do is tell me which gamble you'd rather play.

Step One

Gamble Number 1.   After the election, we will see who the mayor is. If it's the present mayor, you win $100. If it's someone else, you will neither win nor lose anything.

Gamble Number 2.   After the election, we will spin the pointer on this chance wheel, with the wheel set at 90% dark. If the pointer stops in the dark area, you will win $100; if the pointer stops in the light area, you neither win nor lose anything.

Which do you prefer, the first gamble, or the second gamble?

Arthur: I prefer Gamble 2; I'm nearly sure I will win.

Ellen: What do you mean by "nearly sure"?

Arthur: There's 90 chances out of 100 to win.

Ellen: Can I infer from this that the mayor's chances of reelection are smaller than 90?

Arthur: Sure.

Ellen: Okay, here's another choice between two gambles.

Step Two

Gamble Number 1.   After the election, we will see who the mayor is. If it's the present mayor, you win $100. If it's someone else, you will neither win nor lose anything.

Gamble Number 2. After the election, we will spin the pointer on the chance wheel, this time with the wheel set 10% dark. Now which of these two gambles do you prefer?

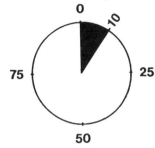

Arthur: On the wheel, there's not much chance of winning. I'd have a better chance to win with the mayor; I'll go with Gamble 1.

Ellen: May I infer that the mayor's chances of reelection are larger than 10?

Arthur: Right.

Ellen: Okay, let's try again.

Step Three

Gamble Number 1. Gamble 1 is on the mayor again. It's the same gamble as in the first two steps.

Gamble Number 2. Again we use the chance wheel, this time set at 50% dark. Which one of these two gambles do you prefer now?

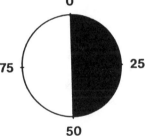

Arthur: I prefer Gamble 2.

Ellen: May I infer that the mayor's chances of reelection are larger than 10 but smaller than 50?

Arthur: Sure.

Step Four

Ellen: Now which do you prefer: Gamble 1 to receive $100 if the mayor wins, or Gamble 2 with the chance wheel set at 25%?.

Arthur: That's a hard one. It's close. I guess I'll go for the mayor, Gamble 1.

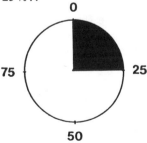

Ellen: So now I'm inferring that you believe the chances for the mayor's reelection are more than 25 but less than 50.

Arthur: Yes, that's right.

Step Five

Gamble Number 1. After the election, we will see who the mayor is. If it's the present mayor, you will get $100. If not, you won't win anything and you won't lose anything.

Gamble Number 2. The chance wheel again, set this time at 30% dark.

Arthur: I have a hard time deciding.

Ellen: Do you have any preference at all? Do you care which gamble you play?

Arthur: I don't know. I just can't choose between them. I really don't care which one I get.

Ellen: So is it reasonable for me to say that the chances that the pointer will stop in the dark area of the circle are the same as the chances you give to the mayor's reelection, 30%?

Arthur: Yes.

Those five steps enable us to elicit a number that expresses Arthur's degree of belief. Arthur felt as if he couldn't express his feelings with a number, but he found he could choose between two gambles. In the end, his choices conveyed to Ellen his degree of belief. This happened at the *indifference point,* when he was indifferent between the two gambles. By the same device, other people could have arrived at different numbers for the same event because they have different beliefs. Although using the chance wheel takes time, it helps in the process of eliciting numbers. Moreover, it enables us to retest a number given offhand.

It may seem that there is no relation whatsoever between an election and the spin of a pointer on the chance wheel. Of course, there is no *content* relation between the two events. The only relation is the degrees of belief associated with the two events. It is easy to give a number to the event of the pointer stopping but more difficult to give a number to the second event. With the help of one, we get a number for the second event; they are identical numbers when we reach the indifference point.

We will not always be willing to give a precise number. It is possible, for example, that Arthur would have stopped before Step 5, saying, "I can't say more than that the chances are between 25 and 50." Sometimes we don't need a precise number; an interval is good enough. Clarity does not call for a *precise* number. An interval is no less clear than a number. As we didn't always require a narrow, ridiculous definition of the problem in the name of clarity (see Chapter 2), we don't always require it here when specifying degrees of belief.

Now, after we have elicited a number, can we justify it? Can we say why "30" or why "between 25 and 50"? Usually we cannot justify the number or the interval in such a way that from the justification we could infer the number (there are some such cases, to be discussed in Chapter 8). We can just state the many reasons that together cause us to feel some degree of belief.

It is not easy to learn a new language. We are all used to speaking in a vague verbal language when expressing degrees of belief. In daily life, this language serves us quite well and the damage caused by its ambiguity is minor, but for important decisions it is helpful to use numbers to express degrees of belief. It may be more difficult to elicit numbers, but it is much more efficient. We understand each other better, numerical expressions are more sensitive to small differences in our feelings, and in the end, in the long run, our decision processes will be better.

Exercises for Section 4.6

1. Try to express in a number the chances you attribute to the event "Our next President will be a Republican."

2. Elicit the chances for the same event from two friends, using the method presented in this chapter. Start with extreme settings of the chance wheel and gradually narrow it down.

II SOME TOOLS

5 Estimation

5.1 INTRODUCTION

A typical situation involving feelings of uncertainty is dealing with a *quantitative problem*. A few examples:

—How many people will come to my party tomorrow night?
—What is the current total number of private cars in the United States?
—What is the shortest driving distance in miles from my house to a specific downtown department store?
—How much will the trip cost?
—How many copies of James Michener's most recent novel will be sold this year?
—How long is the Nile?

Most of us feel uncertain concerning such questions. We are aware of the fact that we do not have the correct answer, namely, the *exact number*. These feelings of uncertainty can be either personal or general (see Chapter 1). They are personal if we feel that this is "our problem"; the number could be found in some reference book (encyclopedia, statistical report, etc.) or there are people who know it (for example, some officials in the Department of Transportation know the total number of private cars in the United States). Maybe even we personally could have found out the exact number, provided that we have had enough time (like measuring the distance from our house to the downtown department store). On the other hand, sometimes our feelings of uncertainty are general: nobody can be sure, for example, how many people will attend your party tomorrow, or what the exact population of Babylon was 3000 years ago.

In the previous chapters we presented several stages for dealing with questions about which we feel uncertain: First, check whether the question is clearly formulated. Second, list different possible answers to it, and third, assign different numbers to the answers describing our different degrees of belief. In such a way, we answer a question and at the same time express the amount of uncertainty that we feel toward it.

Similar rules apply to quantitative problems, where we are frequently interested for practical purposes in getting either a *single number,* which seems to us the closest to the true number, or a *range of numbers,* rather than developing a classification of possibilities and their chances. When reporters, for instance, cover a demonstration, they want to report one number (e.g., approximately 8000 people) or one class (e.g., between 8000 and 10,000 people). These reporters know that the chance of their estimated number being the exact, true number is almost zero. However, a good approximation illustrates the scale of the demonstration; it wasn't a small one in which only a couple of hundred took part, nor was it a huge one in which tens of thousands of people were marching in the streets.

Quite often when we have to assess quantities we feel that we do not have the faintest idea regarding the problem. We feel unable even to tell the appropriate order or magnitude: hundreds, thousands, tens of thousands? Returning to the demonstration example, the street in front of the city hall was full of people participating in the protest. How many were there? It seems as if there is no information available that could enable us to know the size of the crowd. However, if we think a little bit more about the demonstration example and similar problems, by utilizing some methods that will be presented later on in this chapter, we realize that in most cases we do have some *partial or fragmentary information* at our disposal, and it can enable us to make some *assessment or evaluation.* Although it is merely an approximation, it should, in many cases, suffice.

The difficulties we face when assessing such problems are in three areas: (a) we have to *recognize* the fact that we have considerable amounts of partial information concerning many questions; (b) we need to *reveal* the appropriate partial information and to check its relation to the problem under discussion; and (c) finally, we need to *organize* it in such a way that we can utilize it well and eventually reach a good assessment.

In this chapter we will study methods of identifying partial information and deriving a numerical assessment out of it.

5.2 WHAT IS AN ESTIMATE?

A young novelist who has published some books in the past sent a manuscript of a new novel to a publishing house. The publishers read the manuscript and agreed to publish it. Now they have to decide how many copies they should print in the first edition. They cannot be certain exactly how many copies of the first edition will be sold. However, they certainly cannot claim to have no idea because they have some information that may help them assess *approximately* how many copies will be sold, namely, the relevant order of magnitude:

—The publishers have read the manuscript and know what it is about (for instance, this novel describes one of the old families of the South; within this framework a love story is told). They know generally how many copies of similar novels have been sold in the past.

—They are acquainted with the previous books by this novelist and know how many copies of them have sold.

—They know how many copies of a "best-seller" are sold and they believe the new novel will not be a "best-seller."

After the publishers gather and organize all these pieces of information, they will be able to assess the number of copies for printing purposes.

> The procedure for making a numerical assessment based on partial information is called an *estimation procedure.*

The estimation procedure contains two distinct stages:

1. Collecting relevant information on the current problem:
   —Books about old families in the South have, in the past, sold about 8000 copies their first year.
   —The novelist's former books have sold, on average, 2500 copies a year.
   —A "best-seller" usually sells more than 20,000 copies a year.
2. Assembling in some way all these fragments of information in order to obtain an estimate.

> The number obtained by the estimation procedure is called an *estimate.*

Exercises for Section 5.2

1. Following is a list of professions. Give some examples of estimation problems that these people have to solve in connection with their daily work.

—Plumber
—Carpenter
—Truck driver
—Construction worker
—Tourist guide
—Dressmaker
—Film producer
—Housekeeper
—Intelligence officer

2. Describe five cases in which you have made estimates.

5.3 SEARCHING FOR RELEVANT INFORMATION

John's exam will take place two weeks from today. John is wondering how many days before the exam he should start preparing for it. Does he have any information relevant to this problem that may help him to decide when to start studying? Certainly this will not be his first exam; he knows approximately how many days he has spent for preparation in the past for exams of a similar scale and importance. He remembers also whether the preparation time was usually enough or whether sometimes he had the feeling that he still needed more time to cover all the material, or conversely, whether he felt that he had started preparing for the exam so early that by the time of the exam he had forgotten some vital details. In sum, his personal experience with similar exams is definitely relevant information that he can use to obtain the desired assessment.

A couple of students decided to earn some money by selling soft drinks to people celebrating the coming Fourth of July. How many bottles should they buy? They do not have personal experience, but they have several alternative sources for collecting relevant information:

—In the city center there are booths that regularly sell drinks and refreshments. The owners of these booths may furnish information concerning sales of cold drinks on regular weekdays and weekends.

—Perhaps some of these booths sold drinks last Fourth of July and they may remember the quantities sold then.

—Our students can ask themselves and others how many bottles of cold drinks a person who stays in the streets at this time of year will normally consume.

Pieces of information at our disposal and those we successfully collect are *basic data* to use in estimation. Therefore, it is important that they be as accurate as possible. It is sometimes hard to ensure that all pieces of information will be accurate. We normally prefer to use a piece of information in which we are more confident than another piece that we trust less, even though the latter may seem to us to contribute more to the final estimate.

For most of the quantitative problems that we face in our daily lives we do not have accurate information; thus we cannot solve them feeling absolutely confident in our solution. Nevertheless, we almost always have some partial information that can help us obtain an assessment. While thinking about these problems for the first time, we do not always realize we have such information (for instance, we have no idea how many bottles of drink were sold last Fourth of July). But further thinking in other directions will reveal partial information that may help us in our assessment process. We may think, for instance, of the average quantity of bottles consumed by somebody who stays out all day in hot weather.

> It is highly important: (a) to seek actively and persistently after relevant information and (b) to pursue it in different channels and directions.

We can seek information by consulting source books or experts and by thinking hard enough to reveal what partial information we already know. Even if there is not enough time to consult outside sources or experts, it is rarely the case that we find, after some thought, that we have *no* partial information:

> How many tons of apples were picked last year in Oregon orchards?
> What is the weight of the White House?
> What is the total length of all the blood vessels in our body?

For these and similar questions we may have to admit that we have no idea at all, but we should not overuse such claims of lack of knowledge; usually we can think of some way of approaching the estimate.

5.4 PROCESSING PARTIAL INFORMATION—THE ASSESSMENT PROCEDURE

The relevant information furnishes us with basic data. How can we make use of such information? How can we process it to reach a numerical estimate? There are several methods for doing this. These methods differ in the thought processes involved. Following are several illustrations.

Example A.   The organizing committee of the coming convention of Korean War veterans wishes to know the number of people who will attend the convention next year. This information is important to the organizers, for they have to order adequate facilities, parking, food, programs, and so on. How can the members of the committee estimate this number? They decide that they will base their estimate on the number of participants at the last convention, which was held five years ago. This information serves as a starting point to use in constructing the estimate. They consider in what respects the coming convention will be different from the last one. For example, the season (summer vs. fall), publicity, celebrities and entertainers who are expected to arrive, and so on. Based on such partial information the committee decides that 25% more people will attend this year than attended the last convention.

In this example, the committee chose as its starting point a number that they knew accurately. Often, however, the starting point is itself an estimate, which is then adjusted according to the specific conditions of the problem. The choice of a starting point depends in part upon what aspect of the problem is known with the greatest accuracy. In our example, had not the organizers of the convention known how many people attended the last convention, they might have chosen another starting point, perhaps the total number of members of the organization.

One of the methods for estimation is to begin with a starting point and to modify it according to the specific conditions of the problem under discussion.

Example B.   A platoon commander in the Air Force is ordered to prepare an airstrip for emergency use so that light airplanes can land and take off from it. He has to notify his superiors how much time he will need for this task or, in our terminology, he is supposed to estimate the duration of the operation.

The commander, who personally has never before directed such an operation, recalls that the longest duration for a similar operation was a full month. That operation was directed by one of his friends, who was scolded by his superiors for taking much too long.

On the other hand, our platoon commander remembers hearing that such an operation was completed by a platoon in three days during wartime. Therefore, he believes that his assignment would take between 3 and 30 days.

He now considers the specific conditions: the platoon is on peacetime status; there is no need for exceptionally speedy action. But it is summer now, and the area is generally flat, so the operation can be carried out quite quickly. Bearing all these data in mind, the commander can estimate how many days, more or less, he will need for executing this order.

Example C. What is the aerial distance between San Francisco and Wichita? It is definitely less than the distance from San Francisco to New York, but certainly more than the distance from San Francisco to Salt Lake City.

If we have estimates for the distances to New York and Salt Lake City, we have a range of numbers within which the desired estimate will be. We can shrink this range further by seeking more information (perhaps we realize we know the distance between San Francisco and Chicago, and this may serve us as a more suitable upper limit, less extreme than New York).

> Another procedure is to select two extreme values. Within these two boundaries, considering the specific conditions, estimate the desired number.

The extreme values in this second kind of procedure can also serve as the end points of classes of possibilities, whenever we want to construct such classes rather than using a single estimate. In contrast, in the first procedure we try to identify the most plausible class or even a certain number within that class. In this respect the two procedures are essentially different.

Example D. Two foreign correspondents, Jack and Susan, are watching an IDF (Israeli Defense Forces) parade. They get to wondering how many women soldiers serve in the IDF.

Jack: What do you think the number is?

Susan: How could I know? That's classified information.

Jack: I'd like to write an article about the women soldiers in Israel. Let's try to estimate how many there are.

Susan: How can you figure it out?

Jack: It seems quite simple. There are some 3 million Jews in Israel. Half of them are female, so there are about 1.5 million Jewish women in Israel. The average life expectancy for women is about 70 years. In every age group there are, therefore, approximately 20,000 women, because 1.5 million divided by 70 is around 20,000 (assuming, of course, the same number of women in each age group). Regular military service lasts for two years. Thus, at any given point in time, there are about 40,000 women soldiers in the army, in two age groups, 18–19 and 19–20.

Susan: Wait a minute, you don't mean that all the women aged 18 or 19 serve in the army? This number seems to me exaggerated.

Jack: Okay, I'll deduct from my estimate a quarter of the women, who do not serve for various reasons. Therefore, my final estimate is about 30,000 women soldiers in the Israeli army.

Example E.   A tourist and a resident of Los Angeles are talking.

Tourist: I envy you. The weather in Los Angeles is splendid; it hardly ever rains here. In London it rains almost every day the year around.

Resident: Although we do not have as much rain as you have in London, there are plenty of rainy days in L.A. during the year.

Tourist: What are you talking about? I bet there are no more than 5 rainy days during the entire year.

Resident: Let's agree that a rainy day means at least 0.01 inch of rain during the 24–hour period. It rains in L.A. only from October until April. Rain in other months is very rare, so we can ignore that period. There are 7 months of rain, and now let's break it down: (a) in October and in April there are few rainy days, say, about 3 days a month; (b) in the other months, too, not every day is rainy. Let's suppose that in each of these months, there are 5 rainy days on the average. So from November until March we have some 25 (5 multiplied by 5) rainy days. In sum, there are about 31 rainy days during the year in L.A. Obviously, if the year is either very rainy or unusually dry, our estimate will change.

Tourist: I am still envious. If I do the same calculation for London weather, I believe the figure will be around 150 rainy days a year.

Examples D and E illustrate a procedure whereby an estimate is constructed from partial or even full information about related events. Sometimes it is easier to begin with the whole, or with a large number (like the entire Israeli Jewish population, as in Example D), and to obtain by computation one component of that whole, a smaller number that is our goal (e.g., the number of women soldiers). In other circumstances we know something about the components (the number of rainy days in each month, as in Example D) and through them we figure out the whole, the large number that we are trying to estimate (the total sum of rainy days in a typical year).

These two methods are usually called "decomposition" and "recomposition."

> Using the method of *decomposition,* we start with some whole estimate and by computations obtain the desired component.
>
> Using the method of *recomposition,* we estimate components and by computations combine them to get the desired whole.

We have discussed four methods, each of which emphasizes a slightly different procedure for reaching the desired estimate. It should be stressed that:

a. These methods are not *totally* different, so we will not always be able to state clearly that we utilized one of the four methods. Possibly our specific method will be a mixture of two or more of them.

b. It is often a good idea to apply two or more methods.

c. When you deal with estimates, you will certainly find additional methods that were not mentioned here. The type of problem and kind of information available to you will lead you to an appropriate method. Thus the word "methods" is perhaps too formal; these methods should be used merely as recommendations.

Although the methods discussed differ, they share something in common: the estimate is based on a *detailed and explicit procedure.* The partial information is specified and so are the ways by which it is processed. These methods differ from the common practice of estimating and assessing "off-hand" without thinking about the available partial information nor the best way to utilize it.

5.5 ADVANTAGES OF DETAILED AND EXPLICIT ESTIMATION PROCEDURES

Detailed and explicit procedures as described in Section 5.4 will probably produce better estimates in the sense that the estimates will usually be closer to the true number than will vague and inexplicit estimates. The reasons for this are:

a. When we specify the details, we spend more time thinking about the various aspects of the problem.

b. The details enable us to examine the extent to which we are familiar with the data needed for solving the problem, how much of the desired information we already have, and what we still need. In this way we have some criteria to judge the reliability of the estimate we produce.

c. The detail helps reveal those items about which we have considerable amounts of information and therefore can use in the estimation procedure. For example, we have more knowledge about the number of rainy days in our area each month than about the total number the year around. This is why an attempt to tackle the problem as a whole (total number of rainy days annually) will probably result in less accurate estimates than those produced by way of looking at the details on which we have more knowledge (number of rainy days each month).

d. An additional advantage to reaching an estimate by a detailed and explicit way over an "off-hand" estimate is that the former is more open to scrutiny and criticism than the latter. The average number of rainy days each month, the constancy of this number across several months, the month with the highest precipitation, these matters and similar ones are debatable and open to scrutiny. Thus, we can examine the basis for different estimates of the "annual total number of rainy days in L.A." Without such detail it is more difficult to debate or to check the final estimate (as when the tourist in Example E estimated only 5 rainy days a year). Similarly, teachers of mathematics will usually prefer fully described solutions over solutions that give only the answer. The detailed procedure can be scrutinized and corrected much more efficiently than the final numerical result.

Exercises for Sections 5.4 and 5.5

1. Suggest one way to obtain each of the following estimates using the methods of decomposition or recomposition. Describe the various components in detail, but do not make any numerical computations.

 a. How many rooms are there in the Plaza Hotel in New York?
 b. What was the total number of touchdowns scored by the University of Michigan football team last season?
 c. How many words (including repeats) are there in the Bible?
 d. What is the total number of left-handed people nationwide?
 e. If all Ohio's residents stood side by side holding hands, would they succeed in encompassing the state's borders?

2. A test lab checks the reliability of various commercial products. The testing method is illustrated by the following example: If the lab is requested to approve the durability of a certain cloth, say, over 100 washings, it will actually wash a sample of this cloth 100 times and check any deterioration of quality. Now, for the following commercial products, please estimate the number of actions (for instance, washings) that the test lab will have to carry out in order to prove the durability over *five years* of use.

 a. Products intended for use in a house occupied by 4 persons:
  —a front door key. A single testing action will be one locking and one unlocking.
  —a lavatory flushing system
  —an electric light for a kitchen stove
  —an electric wall switch

    b. A ballpoint pen in use by a high school student (testing criterion would be the length in feet of continuous written line).

    c. A small pump for bike tires.

3. Some arithmetic aspects of modern living:

    a. How many films have you watched in your life?

    b. How much money does an average smoker spend for cigarettes during a lifetime?

    c. What is the total number of hours an average college student sits in the classroom before graduation?

    d. How many steps do you make when walking from the parking lot to your desk?

    e. What is the total number of eggs you have consumed so far?

5.6 CHECKING THE ESTIMATE

Checking the estimate is an important part of the estimation procedure. It is customary to differentiate between two kinds of checking, *preliminary* and *detailed.*

Preliminary check.   We will check whether the estimate is plausible. For instance, imagine a candidate becoming excited in an election campaign and exclaiming: "Thirty million men are unemployed." The objective of making the preliminary check is to see whether this figure seems plausible. If there are about 1.5 million men in each age group in the U.S. then there are about 75 million men between the ages of 20 and 70 (see Example D in section 5.4). It is absurd to suppose that almost half of them are unemployed.

Detailed check.   This form of checking is more detailed than the former one in that we are not content with questioning the reasonableness of a given estimate, but actually make new estimates in one or more different ways. Then we compare the new estimate or estimates with the original. If the original estimate seems to us to be unreasonable, we can now reach a more plausible one.

    The estimation procedure is based, as was mentioned before, on partial information and logic. The amount of partial information concerning a given problem differs between people. Somebody knows more and some others know less about it. Somebody may be familiar with one aspect of it while his or her friend is more acquainted with another aspect, and there may be a third person who is familiar with more than one aspect of the matter. Various aspects of the problem, therefore, help the person or persons involved to carry on the estimation procedure in different ways.

The following is an illustration of a detailed check:

> The city engineer is asked to estimate how long it will take to perform some base construction work on a specific road. The reason for this request is that her superiors want to know in advance how long the road will be closed to traffic. The engineer is trying to recall how long it usually takes to do the same work, and accordingly reaches an estimate (here she utilizes the first estimation procedure: starting from some base and modifying it). The engineer knows this is only an estimate and an error might have occurred (an error is likely when dealing with any estimate). The important thing is that the error should not be too large. Accordingly, she checks herself by estimating the same figure differently. She estimates the average time duration of each stage of the whole job and then combines all the estimates (recomposition). Computing the estimates in different ways may reveal biases and errors. If the two estimates are similar, it is likely that the error is small. However, if they are very different, it may mean that one of them or both of them are highly biased; the engineer should review all the stages of estimation to see where the problem might lie.

Preliminary checking and detailed checking can be closely related. For example, having decided quickly that there can't be as many as 30 million unemployed men, we can use the same framework to arrive at a new, more detailed, estimate: "There are about 75 million men between the ages of 20 and 70; if about 10% of them are unemployed, then there are about 7.5 million unemployed men." An estimator more knowledgeable about such demographics would make an even more detailed estimate that includes teenagers with their much higher rates of unemployment, and so forth.

Each kind of checking can be either *personal*—the estimator checks his or her own estimate—or *interpersonal*—the estimate is checked by someone else. The city engineer mentioned above made a personal check by recomputting her original estimate using a different method. This could have been done, of course, as an interpersonal check by another person.

To the greatest extent possible, we should try to avoid letting our estimate depend on the estimation procedure. There is always *one* true value that we are trying to estimate. We wish to obtain more or less similar estimates (that is, practically *one* estimate) of this value by making use of different methods for computing these estimates.

In this chapter, we realize the close connection between uncertainty (which was discussed in Chapter 1) and partial knowledge. For most of the daily problems we solve, we have only partial, rather than full, knowledge. That is why we feel uncertain when dealing with these problems. We have illustrated that there are more and less clever routes for utilizing the partial information available.

We have stressed, as we did in the first chapter, that clever estimation procedures cannot guarantee correct answers. However, the importance of estimation procedures lies in *increasing the chances* of a value that is close to the true one.

Exercises for Section 5.6

1. Perform preliminary checks on the following estimates; are they plausible?

  a. In Hungary there are 450 public telephones.
  b. It takes a steamship 80 days to circle the globe.
  c. One million copies of the New York Times are printed every day.
  d. There are 100 industrial accidents in New York City each year.
  e. If all Pennsylvania's residents stood one on top of the other, the line would reach the moon.

2. For the following questions, try to reach an estimate in two different ways. Are your two estimates close? If not, improve one or both of them.

  a. What is the total number of babies born each day in your state?
  b. What is the total annual mileage of all the motorized vehicles in your state?
  c. How many books have been published in the world this year (including additional printings of old books)?
  d. How many churches are there in the United States?

6 Sampling—Part I

6.1 INTRODUCTION

The *New York Times,* December 20, 1988
New Show Big Hit
The new TV show, "M*A*S*H in World War III," is
proving to be more popular than expected. A public opinion
survey of 2000 respondents revealed by the network today
showed that 60% of those surveyed reported knowing of and
liking the program.

—Katherine: It's no wonder that most of the country likes this program. I
think it's good, too.

—William: Who says that most Americans like this program? The news
story says only 2000 people participated in the survey. Should I remind you
that the total population is over 200 million?

This news item introduces an additional method to reach an estimate
based on partial information. Here, partial information is obtained from a
sample that is only a portion of the population that interests us. The sample
is the source of the information.

Nobody can be absolutely confident that exactly 60% of the *entire
population* (about 210 million people) like that program. However, 60% of
the 2000 respondents is certainly an *estimate* of the percentage of those who
like the program in the entire population. We do not have *full information*

about the opinion of all the people, because they were not asked. The information concerning these 2000 who were asked is *partial,* and may serve as an estimate for the population as a whole.

We frequently hear about estimates based on samples:

Many public opinion polls are held before elections, in an attempt to estimate the voting results. Such a poll is based on small samples of voters who are asked about their voting intentions. The election results are then inferred from the results of the poll.

When *Time* magazine is interested in knowing the opinion of the public on new economic policies, for instance, it sponsors a survey of a sample of the public and then relies on the estimate obtained by the survey results.

Testing labs that check the question of new commercial products usually conduct tests on samples of the products; the results serve as an estimate of the quality of the product in general.

Also, we ourselves often experience making estimates based on samples:

—Mary: Did you see that bus driver? He is so discourteous. He closes the bus doors before the last passenger touches the ground, and he does not reply politely to the passengers' questions.

—Jane: He is not the only one. Yesterday I had a similar experience with another bus driver.

—Mary: Bus drivers in this city are so rude!

—Laurie: Look, Bob, what a beautiful display window. Aren't those clothes beautiful?

—Bob: Yeah. Let's go in; this store sells great things.

—Tom: Dan, I'm going to see "Black Storm." Do you want to come with me?

—Dan: Who told you that film is any good?

—Tom: I saw a small bit of it in a preview. It was fascinating. I assume the entire film is like that.

In all these cases, evaluation was made on the basis of partial information. This information was obtained from a sample:

Mary and Jane assume all city bus drivers are rude by observing only two of them. For Jane and Mary, these two bus drivers constitute a sample representing all the others.

Laurie and Bob believe the store sells attractive clothes just by observing its display window. The displayed merchandise serves as a sample of the entire stock in the store.

Tom decides that the film is interesting because he was fascinated by the portion he watched.

Even this small list of examples shows that in some instances it is justified to infer from a sample of items to the whole set from which it was originally sampled. However, in other cases, such inferences are not justified. There are samples that look "good" and reliable; others seem "bad." In this chapter we will learn something about samples in order to know when we can trust an estimate based on them. Nevertheless, we should keep in mind that although the sample may be good and reliable, the information derived from it is partial and no more than an estimate. As in any other situation involving uncertainty, we cannot be sure what the true situation is. Unless we check the whole relevant group, we will remain, to some extent, uncertain, even with the best of samples.

6.2 POPULATION AND SAMPLE

A major city is considering repaving a road often used by trucks to bypass the city. To determine how thick the new paving should be, the city planning office is interested in finding out what proportion of all the traffic on this road during the year is trucks. How can such an investigation be conducted? Obviously, the city will not hire a group of people to watch the highway a whole year, 24 hours a day, and count all vehicles driven on it. Such a procedure would consume too much time, funds, and personnel. Instead, a sampling procedure is used.

A certain short period is selected, during which all vehicles on the road, trucks as well as other vehicles, are counted. In such a way, we get a *partial group* of the total number of vehicles using the road. The percentage of trucks in this group is computed and this percentage serves as an estimate for the same percentage in the total group.

Which partial group should be chosen? There are several alternatives:

a. The city could decide to count the vehicles during a *single day* in that year. Thus the percentage of trucks in that day will be the estimate for the annual percentage.

b. It is possible to choose *one day each month,* so the partial group will be all vehicles on the road on these 12 days.

c. All vehicles on the road during *one week* could serve as a partial group.

d. Still another period for counting the vehicles could be *one hour every day in the year.*

Each one of these (and other) partial groups is a *sample* of the larger group of vehicles using the road throughout the year. This large group, of which the percentage of trucks is our objective, is called the *population.*

The population is the sum total of items on which we want to obtain information.

A sample is a partial group of items selected from the population.

Sampling is the procedure of selecting a sample from the population.

Not all populations are people. You can say "the population of VW Rabbits" or "the population of all bottles in a food store" as well as "the population of our town."

As we have seen, various partial groups, that is, various samples, can be selected. Figure 6.1 illustrates three different samples drawn from the same population. There are, of course, many different samples, varying in size of sample or observed features, that could be drawn from this population.

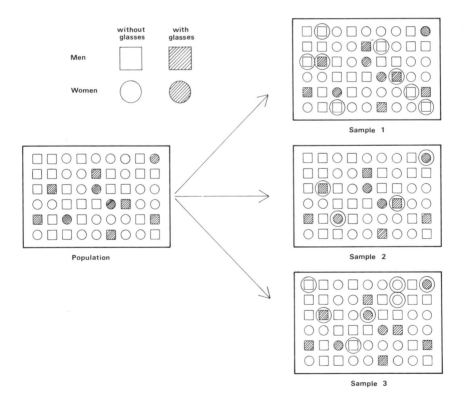

FIG. 6.1   Three samples from one population.

Figure 6.1 demonstrates several features:

1. Every item in the sample is part of the relevant population.
2. Not every item of the population is included in the sample (unless the entire population is included, and in such a rare case, it is no longer called a sample). Thus, a sample is always a subgroup of the relevant population.
3. There are many ways by which samples from a population may be drawn. The samples can differ in composition (different items) and in size (number of items).

As far as the population is concerned, the information derived from a sample is always partial and serves as an estimate of a certain quantity of the population. The percentage of trucks among all vehicles driven on the road during a single day is used as an estimate of the annual percentage; the percentage of people interested in a TV program, assessed in a sample of 2000 respondents, serves as an estimate of the percentage of the entire population of TV watchers.

Exercises for Section 6.2

Go back to the exercises in Chapter 5. From them, select 5 estimation problems for which a sample would be helpful, and plan a sampling procedure. For each:

a. What was the population of interest?
b. What was the feature of interest?
c. What was the sample you have chosen?

6.3 WHEN TO USE A SAMPLE

When information on a certain population is needed, the surest way is to check the entire population. But such an approach is usually impractical and sometimes even impossible:

1. *When the relevant population is very large.*
For example, scientists want to learn about the composition of the moon's soil. It is impossible to check the entire soil of the moon. Instead, samples of it are investigated.
2. *When the costs (money, time, or personnel) involved in checking the whole population are too high.*
—Counting all the vehicles using a given road during the whole year is a costly task in terms of research crew and time involved.

—Testing the efficiency of a new medicine on the entire population of people who suffer from a specific disease will be enormously expensive; quantities of professional workers, sophisticated equipment, facilities and time would be required. Moreover, such a large-scale testing is almost impossible because some people do not know they suffer from the specific disease, others are hard to locate, and still others would not agree, for various reasons, to serve as "guinea pigs."

In such cases, it is more practical and convenient to use a sample.

3. *Sometimes a portion of the relevant population is inaccessible.*

—A hospital wishes to assess the differences in body weight between male and female babies. The entire relevant population consists of all babies born recently, those who are born right now, and those who will be born in the future. How can babies not yet born be checked?

4. In some instances, *the testing procedure either destroys or alters the tested items.* Testing the entire population, therefore, will result in total destruction.

—A manufacturer of matches has recently received complaints from customers that their matches tend to break when struck. The company wants to check the strength of the matches that are now being packed for shipment. Testing their strength by striking all of them would destroy an entire shipment. Therefore, testing a sample is a better idea.

—A testing lab is asked to check the durability of some glass cookware that is supposed to be heat resistant. The lab intends to check the maximum temperature that this cookware can stand. The testing procedure will be to heat the product and keep a continuous record of its condition at different levels of heat until it fails. Obviously, such a destructive testing procedure cannot be performed on all the factory's line of cookware. Instead, only a sample can be subjected to such testing.

In sum, we have seen that in many cases a sample is the best way to get an estimate of a certain phenomenon in a total population.

6.4 WHAT IS A GOOD SAMPLE?

Using a sample instead of checking the entire population is, as we have seen, common and sometimes even indispensable. We have also seen that various samples can be selected from the same population. Thus we must now ask:

1. What is a good sample?
2. How can such a sample be chosen from the population?
3. Given certain results based on a sample, to what extent can we rely on that sample?

Let us deal with the first question. The result obtained by checking a sample (for instance, the percentage of trucks out of all vehicles driven on a road *during a week*) serves as an estimate of the similar result in the population as a whole (the same percentage during *the whole year*).

The estimate obtained from a sample is better to the extent that it is close to the true figure (which can be obtained, in principle, if the entire population is tested). *Therefore, a good sample is one which provides a good estimate.* Such a sample is called a *representative sample,* namely, the estimate obtained from it represents, or reflects, the relevant feature in the entire population.

—Let us assume that 52% of the whole population like the TV program "M*A*S*H in World War III" (of course, the percentage of the entire population is actually *unknown,* and that is why we need a sample). To the extent that the percentage of interested respondents in our sample is close to 52%, the sample is more representative and the estimate derived from it is better (in the sense that it is closer to the true value).

A good sample is representative; it reflects the entire population regarding the feature of interest.

We choose a sample in order to avoid investigating the entire population. Therefore, we cannot judge whether or not a sample is representative of the feature of interest by comparing its results to those of the population. We infer from the sample to the population, rather than compare the former with the latter.

So *how* can we ensure in advance, or at least increase the chances, that the sample we choose will be representative regarding the feature of interest? We are dealing now with the question, *how does one select a good sample?*

In the following example it is easy to choose a good sample:

—A researcher wants to know the hair color of the members of an African tribe. Suppose it is known that all members of the tribe have the same hair color. Then the researcher will be satisfied with a sample of one tribe member; this person serves as a sample representing the entire tribe.

In this example, the population of concern (all the tribe members) is *homogeneous with respect to the investigated feature;* one tribe member has the same hair color as any other member of the same tribe. Hence, we can infer the investigated feature from even a very small sample. Any sample that is chosen in this case will be "good" for it is identical in this trait to the entire population. Here, then, the result of any sample tested will be identical to the true value. However, such cases, in which the population is homogeneous in regard to the investigated feature, are rare indeed. In most instances the population is not homogeneous with respect to the feature of interest. Quite often, this lack of uniformity is precisely the core of our interest.

—People's opinion about a TV program is not uniform. We want to learn how many people like the program, how many are indifferent, and how many dislike it.

—Not all the vehicles driven on a road are trucks. The truck percentage is what we need to know to design the repaving.

—In preparation for a possible draft, the army wants to know the height of 18- and 19-year-olds for the purpose of ordering adequate clothing. Obviously there are differences in height; the army wishes to obtain estimates of the percentages of recruits in each height category (for instance, "very tall"—above 6'2"; "tall"—between 5'11" and 6'2"; "average"—between 5'7" and 5'10", etc.).

When the population is not homogeneous, not every sample is a good one.

—A group of men eating lunch in an expensive restaurant discussed the *average annual income* of American men. After a long debate the diners decided to use themselves as a sample. Each one wrote down his annual wages and they calculated the average. This figure served them as an estimate of the average annual income of all American men.

Is this a good estimate? Is the sample selected by the diners representative of all men in the country? Probably not. The entire population includes people with high, medium, and low salaries. Had the sample included men belonging to all these three classes of salary level, there would be a better chance that the estimate derived from it (the average income) would be close to the average in the population. However, because the sample consisted of men having lunch in an expensive restaurant, it is reasonable to assume that they were all well-to-do people. Therefore, this sample cannot be regarded as representative of the whole population and an estimate obtained from it is not a good one (because it will not be close to the true value). This is a *biased sample*.

A biased sample is a sample that does not represent a population with regard to the feature of interest.

When a population is not homogeneous, not every sample will represent it. This is the case in most instances that we are interested in investigating. It is important when dealing with such populations that the samples drawn will be representative. How can we select representative samples? How can we avoid biased ones?

Exercises for Section 6.4

Choose a sample to be used in estimating the percentage of people having the following characteristics in the entire U.S. population. What is a bad sampling method for each characteristic (i.e., a sampling method that will result in a very biased sample)?

The characteristic	*A bad sampling method*
has a telephone	a telephone survey
likes classical music	
is married	
is a Republican	
speaks English fluently	
likes football	
weighs more than 185 lbs.	
teaches at a university	
has fathered one child	
has a high school diploma	

6.5 HOW TO CHOOSE A REPRESENTATIVE SAMPLE

The Department of Education wishes to know what proportion of high school seniors plan to go to college. They hire a research scientist to conduct appropriate research on the topic. This scientist lives in Manhattan, near three private high schools. It is most convenient for her, in terms of time, budget, and accessibility, to choose a sample from the three nearby high schools.

Will such a proposed sample be representative? Will this sample, consisting of the seniors from three Manhattan private schools, represent all U.S. high school seniors on the characteristic, college plans? Probably not; this sample is probably biased.

How can we judge whether the result based on such a sample will be unbiased?

1. First, we asked ourselves whether the potential sample *differs* significantly from the entire population. The answer is affirmative: the population is comprised of high school seniors residing in cities, towns, and rural areas, whereas the proposed sample is made up solely of students in a

metropolitan area. Thus, the sample does not represent the relevant population in connection with the feature "rural/urban." Furthermore, the population contains both public school and private school students, whereas the sample contains only the latter.

2. We then ask whether the features "rural/urban" and "public/private" have some relation to the feature "college plans." In other words, the question is whether city residents differ from town and rural residents and whether public school students differ from private school students in their intentions for college. We believe such differences exist.

3. We assume, then, that there is a high chance that the proposed sample is not representative of the entire population, not only in the features "rural/urban" and "public/private" (which are not of interest at the moment), but also in the research topic "college plans."

We disqualified the Manhattan private school sample because it does not represent the population in two features that we believe are related to the feature of interest. We can use these same considerations to try to select a representative sample, so that we will be able to put more trust in an estimate obtained from it.

Before polling the sample (not afterward) we can think of other characteristics that we believe are related to the feature of interest, and plan a sample that adequately represents these characteristics. Such representation can increase the chances of having a better representation of the feature of interest, and thus of the sample being a good one, in the sense that the estimate will be close to the true value.

What are the characteristics related to "college plans"?

We have already mentioned private versus public schools. We should take this characteristic into account in our sample. If we know that 3% of all U.S. seniors attend private schools, then in a sample of, say, 1000 students, we should include 30 (3%) from private schools and the rest from public schools.

Likewise, we should include in our sample a proportion of city, town, and rural residents; the proportion in the sample should be the same as the proportion in the population of high school seniors.

Other characteristics that we believe are related to college plans spring easily to mind. We list here just a few:

—Parents' education (did one or both of the parents attend college?).
—Parents' income.
—Number of books in the student's home.

There are surely other characteristics linked to college plans, such as sex of the student, number of children in the family, and certain personality traits of the student.

Now, if we want the investigated sample to be similar to the population in all the characteristics linked to the feature of interest, we need to:

—Make an inclusive list of the characteristics we believe are related to the feature of interest.

—Check the proportion of each one of these characteristics in the population.

—Make sure that there will be comparable representation of these characteristics in the sample.

This, as you may have suspected, is impossible. First, it is hard to ensure that we will think of *all* possible important characteristics related to the feature of interest. Some of them we might simply overlook (for instance, the parents' education), whereas there are surely other characteristics that are related to the feature of interest unbeknownst to us.

Second, even if we were to include every possible influencing characteristic, we would not know the proportion of each one in the population. (Examples: How many students' homes have more than 200 books? What is the percentage of students having a high level of self-confidence?)

In order to know all these facts we would have to conduct separate research projects concerning each characteristic, and for that we would need appropriate samples. Thus we face a never-ending requirement for good samples. Therefore, this method is impractical; indeed, it is seldom used.

6.6 RANDOM SAMPLING

There is another, easier, method for dealing with sample problems. It is called the method of *random sampling*. We will first demonstrate this method using the same research example.

—Let us assume that the total number of high school seniors is 3 million. Let us assume further that the research scientist has the college plans of these students on cards, one card per person. These 3 million cards can be shuffled by a gigantic automatic shuffling machine, which can spit out a number of cards after shuffling them.

In order to select a sample of 1000 students, the investigator operates the machine to shuffle them and "deal" 1000 of them. The investigator thus has a sample of 1000 students. What are the features of this sampling method?

a. Each "item" (card, person) has the same chance of being included in the sample as any other item.

b. The chance of a certain item's inclusion in the sample is independent of any other item's chance. That is, whether or not a certain item is included has no influence whatsoever on whether or not any other item will be included, too. This stems from the fact that, due to the shuffling, all possible items of the population are available for selection.

This is random sampling, which is characterized by the fact that *the sole determinant of inclusion in the sample is chance.* Here, then, we cannot know in advance what will be the composition of the sample (for example, how many private school students will be included in it).

Note that such randomness does not exist when we are using the former sampling method. There we determined that, for instance, 30 private school students would be included in the sample. In other words, *we determined in advance the sample constitution,* rather than having it being determined by pure chance. Moreover, if the investigator in this example would indeed base the sample solely on the students at three Manhattan private schools, this approach will be even less random, for not only would public school students have no chance of inclusion in the sample, but also other private school students would be excluded. In other words, the investigator, in fact, determined in advance exactly who would be included.

Another example:

—A school teacher wants to order a certain film for the school's extra-curricular entertainment program. He is interested in knowing the percentage of his school's students who have already seen it. He doesn't want to bother asking every single student whether he or she has seen the film, for that would be time consuming and would interfere with an already busy schedule. The school teacher decides, therefore, to rely on a sample of students. Naturally, he wishes the sample to represent as much as possible the entire student population in regard to the true percentage of those who have seen the film.

If he decides to utilize the first sampling method, he should first think of all the characteristics linked to "has seen/has not seen" the film, and then try to represent them in the sample. Some examples of such characteristics are: class level (seniors have more homework to do than juniors, so they have less time available for going to the movies), residential area (the distance from most movie theaters), possibly gender (if it is a war film, more males may have seen it than females), and so on.

We have already discussed the difficulties involved in this method. If, instead, the school teacher decides rather to use the *random sampling method,* he can use the students' files, decide what will be the sample size, say 100,[1] and then *randomly* select 100 names from the files. For instance, he can throw all the cards in front of a fan and pick up, for his sample, the 100 cards that land closest to the water cooler (this sampling procedure, though ridiculous, is intended to demonstrate again the term "random").

---

[1] We will later discuss various considerations involved in deciding sample size.

> Using the *random sampling method* we select a sample such that:
>
> a. Each item in the population has an equal chance of inclusion in the sample.
>
> b. A particular item's chance of inclusion in the sample is independent of any other item's chance.
>
> A sample selected by this method is called a *random sample*.

When using the first, representative-characteristic method, we were careful to ensure, in the sample, adequate representation of characteristics we believed had some connection to the investigated one. Thus, we were hoping the investigated characteristic would also be represented in the sample, thereby ensuring a good estimate.

Now, after the random sampling method has been introduced, the same basic question applies: "How can we make sure there is adequate representation using this method?" For without representation of various characteristics, the chances are low that the sample will be representative of the investigated characteristic and the estimate will be close to the true value. Using the *first method,* we ensured *beyond doubt* adequate representativeness of such characteristics, claiming that this increases the chances of having adequate representation of the investigated characteristic too. *Using the random method, we cannot ensure anything definitely.* However, as you will soon see, there is a *high chance* that the sample represents the population with respect to all characteristics, including the investigated one, and our gain is that we saved most of the costs involved in implementing the first method.

—There are 1000 small balls in a jar. They are numbered and all are similar in size and shape. Ten of these balls (1%) are red and the rest, 990 (99%) are white. We can draw a random sample of 100 balls by stirring the balls and then drawing out 100 with our eyes closed. What is the chance that such a sample will be made up mostly of red balls (say, 70 red and 30 white)? This chance can be computed, but even without computation we would agree that such a chance is quite small, for most of the balls in the jar are white. Therefore, we would expect that there is a high chance of obtaining a sample in which most of the balls are white.

It is highly improbable that such a sample would be made up of exactly 1% of red balls (that is, 1 such ball) and 99% white balls (99). Yet most of the balls in the sample will be white, and very few (or none) will be red.

—Similarly, if 3% of all high school seniors attend private schools, by sampling 1000 students randomly the chances of getting *exactly* 30 private school students is very small, but we have a good chance of getting approximately 30 private school students and about 970 public school students. The same rule applies to all other characteristics discussed here.

> Utilizing the random sampling method, we expect to obtain an
> approximate representation of all possible characteristics,
> without having to think in advance about all the
> characteristics or to know their proportions in the population.

When researchers use the first sampling method, they usually combine it
with the second one. If, for instance, in our example of high school seniors
the researchers want to *ensure* representation of public/private schools,
they will decide that there will be, say, 30 private school students and 970
public school students (according to the appropriate percentages in the
population). The 30 private school students will be selected randomly from
all private school students and similarly the other 970 will be selected randomly from among the rest. Such a sample is called a *stratified sample*.

Exercises for Sections 6.5 and 6.6

1. In the following table, each cell represents a sample of a particular
characteristic, sampled in a certain way. Write an R in each cell for which
you believe the sampling is representative; write a B if you think the sampling is biased. The population of concern is the entire population of the
country. Explain your answers for each case.

	No. Yrs. School	Blood Type	Height	No. TVs	Gender
1. Sending letters to every 10th address using the files of the AFL-CIO.					
2. Interviewing adults whose Social Security number's last 3 digits are 357.					
3. Interviewing every person who passes by a certain cafe one morning.					
4. Interviewing all Manhattan high school seniors.					
5. Interviewing the parents who attend PTA meetings of 10 elementary schools in Chicago					

2. For every B you marked in the former exercise, write down the largest
population for which it would be proper to make inferences from the sample to the population.

6.7 SAMPLING ERROR

It is implausible that using the random sampling method we will select a sample that *exactly* represents the population in the investigated characteristic (namely, that the estimate obtained from it will be identical to the true value, which would have been computed had we checked the entire population). *There will nearly always be some error.*

—A nurse in a college infirmary wishes to know the average weight of entering freshmen, to compare it with similar data she collected 10 years ago.

a. She can weigh each entering freshman and divide the total weight by the number of students weighed; the result will be the desirable average.

$$\text{The average weight of freshmen} = \frac{\text{Total weight of all freshmen this year}}{\text{Number of students weighed}}$$

Let us assume she did that, and the result she got was 135 lbs. This is the *true value.*

b. She can save time and effort by weighing only a sample of students. Let us suppose she decided to choose 30 students randomly. She weighed them and calculated the average in a similar way:

$$\text{The average weight of 30 students} = \frac{\text{Total weight of the 30 students}}{30}$$

Let us say the average she calculated was 138 lbs.

If the nurse selected another random sample of 30 students, she would get another number, perhaps 127, 145, or maybe 136 lbs. Any number based upon results of a sample will be merely an estimate, and there will usually be error. When she computed the average based on her first sample, she got 138 lbs., a difference of 3 lbs. between this estimate and the true value. If her estimate on another sample was, say, 142 lbs., the error would have been 7 lbs.

> The difference between the estimate and the true value is called sampling error.

Such an error will almost always occur. It stems from the heterogeneity of the population and the fact of sampling, that is, in sampling we check only a portion rather than the whole population.

We cannot guarantee that such an error will not occur, for it is always expected when inferring from a sample to the entire population. However, we will always attempt to minimize the error.

The sampling error will be smaller to the extent that the sample is more representative of the investigated characteristic. How can we ensure a representative sample when sampling randomly? Due to the nature of random sampling we cannot, of course, ensure anything definitely. However: a) random sampling increases the chance that the sample will be representative (in contrast to non-random sampling); and b) the chance that a random sample will be representative increases to the extent that the sample is larger.

What is the connection between *sample size* and *representative sample*?

Imagine that the nurse, who is still interested in the average weight of incoming freshmen, chooses *two* students randomly, weighs them, and computes their average weight. This figure is an estimate of the average weight of all incoming freshmen. But it could happen that the nurse chose either two fat students, the average weight of whom is, say, 180, or two very slim students whose average weight is 80 lbs. These weights, one very high and one very low, are, obviously, bad estimates of the true average weight in the population (135 lbs.), because the sampling errors are so large (45 and 55 lbs.).

It is much less likely that such extreme averages will occur when randomly sampling 30 students, rather than 2. Among these 30, there will probably be some who are heavier than the average (say, 160 or more) and still others who are lighter than the average (say, 105 or less). It is unlikely that the randomly chosen 30 students are all extremely fat or all slim. The heavier than average and the slimmer than average will tend to balance one another, and the total average will be around 135 lbs. It is very likely, therefore, that the sampling error based upon the weights of 30 randomly sampled students will be much smaller than that based on only two students.

This example demonstrates the general rule:

A large sample, selected randomly, increases the chances that the sample is representative, the estimate is good, and the sampling error is small.

As the sample gets larger, the chance of a large error diminishes.

When the sample is actually the entire population, the estimate is equal to the true value and the error will be zero.

Exercises for Section 6.7

Following is a list of 9 populations. For each one:
a. Formulate a question that may interest someone (including you).

b. Point out how you might select a good sample from the population in order to obtain an estimate about the question of interest.

1. The population of chairs manufactured by a specified company.
2. The population of cabbage butterflies.
3. The population of scientists in the U.S.
4. The population of words beginning with the letter H.
5. The population of books printed in the U.S.
6. The population of babies born in California.
7. The population of urban areas in the world.
8. The population of treaties signed in the past among various nations.
9. The population of eighty-year-olds in the U.S.

7 Sampling—Part II

7.1 WHAT IS "SAMPLING FROM MEMORY"?

Think a bit about each of the following questions[1] and suggest an answer for each:

1. Which are more numerous in the English language:
   a. Words beginning with the letter M, or
   b. Words beginning with the letter Q?
2. Which are more numerous in the English language:
   a. Words the third letter of which is R, or
   b. Words beginning with the letter R?

Probably, most of you answered *a* for the first question, and *b* for the second. That is, most of you believe there are more words beginning with M than words beginning with Q and more words beginning with R than words the third letter of which is R.

Before checking the dictionary to see if these answers are correct, let us try to reconstruct the *thinking processes* involved in your attempts to answer these questions.

You probably tried, for the first question, to recall words beginning with M and words beginning with Q. In this short attempt you recalled more of the former than the latter, and this led you to conclude that this is the general situation in the language.

Similarly, you tried to recall words beginning with R and those of which the third letter is R. Because you were able to recall more words beginning with R, you decided that this is the general situation in English.

---

[1]These examples are from Tversky & Kahneman, 1973.

Does this process remind you of something? We hope it reminds you of the sampling issues we discussed in the previous chapter. As there, we are not dealing with the entire population—the complete English vocabulary—but rather with a portion of it: the words which you could recall. That is:

1. We asked about the *population* of words beginning with M and with Q.
2. The desired characteristic was: "words beginning with M" and "words beginning with Q."
3. The answer was based on a sample: Words beginning with M and those beginning with Q that you recalled in a short time.
4. Because most words you recalled were those beginning with M, you inferred that there are more words beginning with this letter than those beginning with Q in the entire language (the population).

This conclusion was based on the sample that you retrieved from memory. The words recalled in that short period served as a sample representing the population as a whole. The situation is similar for the second question. Try to specify the population, the characteristic, and the sample for it.

Note that these two samples were not selected from a newpaper, a book, or a dictionary, but rather were created internally by thinking. Which items were included in these samples? Each word having the desired characteristic that you recalled during a short time.

Sampling from memory yields a sample of items that one recalls during a specified period of time.

This is certainly not the first time you have sampled from memory. This form of sampling is common when one is attempting to estimate quantities in uncertain situations. Examples:

—Which are more frequent on U.S. roads, GM or Ford cars? If asked this question, you will probably try to recall cars belonging to friends, acquaintances, neighbors, and so on, and you will infer from this sample to the general situation.

—Which are more frequent in the U.S., families having two children, or those having one? Again, you will search your memory, and if among the people you know there are more families having two children you will conclude that this is the situation in the entire population.

Is this "sampling from memory" procedure a "good" one? A "correct" one? Does it qualify in terms of the principles of good sampling discussed before?

7.2 DOES "SAMPLING FROM MEMORY" PRODUCE GOOD SAMPLES?

In the appendix to this chapter (on page 96) there is a name list of various people. Read the whole list once (now, before reading beyond this paragraph) and return to this page. Please have a pencil and paper ready.

This list serves as the population. The question which we are interested in is: Are there more men or women in the list (in the population)? (Please *do not* reread the list yet.)

Now, write down the sampling you did just now in your mind. Write down all the names of the men and women that you can recall from that list. Do it quickly; do not spend more than half a minute on this task.

Now look at the list that you wrote. Are there more men than women in it? In former experiments dealing with this task it was found that most of the subjects (high school and college students as well as older people) recalled and wrote down more women's names than men's names. Hence, these subjects concluded that there are more women's names in the original list. How about you? Did you draw the same conclusion on the basis of the list of names you recalled?

If you now check the original list you will see that those of you who decided that it contains more women's names were wrong. There are more men's names on it.

We have said before that a good sampling procedure may lead to a bad result (a sample not representative of the entire population) and thus a biased estimate. Nevertheless, it is surprising that *most* people tend to recall, in this case, an "unrepresentative" sample (most of us recall more women's names than men's names, contrary to the men/women ratio in the original list). Why did most of us produce a biased sample? In order to understand the reasons for that, let us consider sampling from memory in the light of the sampling principles discussed in the previous chapter.

We have said that in order to increase the chances of the selected sample being representative of the population we ought to ensure the following two principles:

1. That the items will be sampled randomly.
2. That many items will be selected (the sample will not be too small).

In the former chapter we presented some methods by which one can sample randomly, like drawing cards with eyes closed, using a shuffling machine, and so on. We will check now whether sampling from memory is a "random" sampling procedure. Does it satisfy the two principles mentioned before? In other words: (a) does every one of the items have the same chance of being recalled? and (b) is the chance of recalling any one item independent of the chance of every other item?

7.3 DOES EVERY ITEM HAVE THE SAME CHANCE OF BEING RECALLED?

The Availability Principle

In the very first example in this chapter, we asked which are more numerous in English: words beginning with the letter M or words beginning with Q. We based our answer on the sample of words we could recall.

When trying to answer that question, did each word beginning with M and each one beginning with Q have the same chance of being recalled? Did every word have the same chance, or were there some words that had no chance at all? There are, for sure, some words that we do not know, words that we have never used in our vocabulary, for they are very rare in daily language use (examples: meristic, miniver, quadrat, and quartan). The chances of such totally unfamiliar words being recalled are practically zero, no matter how much effort we put into our thinking.

Hence, this is a situation where *we actually did not sample from the total population, but rather from a portion of it*. If there are words that have no chance of recall, the principle "every item has the same chance of being recalled" is violated.

We can probably think of situations where we sample in our memory from the *entire* population. In such cases, does every item have the same chance of being sampled? Let us check that experimentally.

The following is a list of words. Please read it once and then cover it up.

cold, bolide, enol, nice, warm, gavial, akee, friend, foin, girl, picture, scop

Now write down all the words you remember. Which of the words do you remember easily? Naturally, the ones that are familiar (cold, nice, warm, friend, girl, picture). These are more easily recalled than the unfamiliar (bolide, enol, gavial, akee, foin, scop). Thus, familiar words are more *available* in memory. Generally, a highly familiar thing or event that we have been repeatedly exposed to is more *available* in our memory; its chances of being recalled are greater.

> There are items in our memory that are more *available* than others, that is, items having a greater chance of being recalled than other items.

Therefore, even if we sample from the *entire population,* not every item has the same chance of being remembered. For that reason *sampling from memory is not random.*

Let us review again the list in the appendix. We now can see why we were able to remember more women's names than men's names, that is, why our sample was biased. For the purpose of demonstration, the list was compiled to include names of very famous women, whereas the men listed are less well known. When asked to recall these, we were able to remember more women than men, because being better known increased their recall chances in comparison with the men's chances.

> Familiar, well-known, and prominent items are more available in memory than items not having these qualities.

Another feature of memory is demonstrated here. If we return to the original list and the recalled one, we will realize that it is easier to recall both the beginning and the end of it than the middle, that is, the items at both extremes are more easily recalled than the middle items. Several explanations have been offered for this phenomenon. Some researchers think that fewer factors interfering with recall exist for both the first item on the list (before which there are no items) and the last one (after which there are none). In contrast, the middle items interfere with each other. Others believe we are more attentive to the first and the last word of a list than to words in the middle of a list. Still others say that the last words in a list are closer in time to the start of recalling the list so they "do not have time" to be forgotten.

The fact that we recall recent items is familiar to us. Usually we remember many more events that occurred recently (a few hours or days ago) than things that happened long ago (provided that they all share more or less the same importance to us). However, highly important, impressive or well-known events that occurred in our remote past will still be recalled eventually.

This feature of memory—the tendency to recall initial and, even more, recent things—means, in the present context, that the chances of recall are not equal for all of the items.

> Items that were first or last in a certain context are more available in memory than other items.

We return now to the two questions presented at the start of this chapter. Were your answers correct?

When answering the first question, you decided that there are more words beginning with the letter M than words beginning with the letter Q. This is correct (compare the number of pages of M words in any English dictionary with Q words). If all the words beginning with M and those beginning with Q were equally known and familiar to us, they all had the same chance, more or less, of being recalled. Given that in the English language there are, in fact, more words beginning with M, no wonder we recalled more of these than those beginning with Q and then drew the correct conclusion.

Now, regarding the second question, it is incorrect to say that there are more words beginning with R than those in which R is the third letter. There are more words of the second type. Why were we mistaken; why did we create a biased sample? Why did our memory in this case fail us, that is, why did we recall more words beginning with R than words with R as the third letter?

It did not happen because our knowledge of the English language is imperfect. It happened because of the method we use to think of instances for the sample. It is relatively easy to search for a word beginning with a certain letter. Usually we pronounce that letter and try to add various other vowels and consonants to it until we construct a meaningful word. It is much harder to do this when looking for words in which a certain letter appears in the third position. (Try to do this and you will realize the difficulty.) Here, again, not every word has an equal chance of being recalled (that is, being included in the sample).

The method we use for searching our memory affects which items are recalled. Sometimes that method is chosen for convenience, as when we try to form M words by thinking "ma . . .", "me . . .", and so on. But there are a variety of factors that determine the search method we use, including beliefs and wishes.

Instead of checking a *random* sample for the purpose of ascertaining the truth of a specific hypothesis or belief that we hold (for example, to see whether in random samples of Scots and Irish the percentage of miser Scots is higher than the percentage of miser Irish), our belief itself dictates the contents of the sample: we quite easily remember instances confirming our belief and hardly ever remember instances disconfirming it, even if the hypothesis is, in fact, false. If we strongly believed that the Irish were more miserly than the Scots, we would find it easy to remember instances confirming that view; it would be more difficult to find contradicting ones.

This tendency of recalling mostly confirming instances is one of the roots of prejudice, stereotypes, and incorrect images people hold in connection with other nations, ethnic groups, and so on.

Obviously, we cannot always base our generalizations on extensive scientific studies of the entire population, but at least we ought to base our beliefs on random samples, rather than sampling instances from our memory, which is biased toward confirming our beliefs.

> Items that confirm our hypothesis are more easily recalled
> than items that contradict it.

Another reason that some items are recalled easily is because they are vivid, dramatic, or emotionally laden.

Is it true that most bus drivers in the city are discourteous? People who hold this view will be deeply impressed by any impolite reply of a bus driver and will remark, "Another rude bus driver." They may tell this to friends or even write a letter about it to a local newspaper. Each such event will be very well remembered. However, numerous other cases of riding the bus without encountering rudeness are forgotten because they are not dramatic or vivid; nothing happened worth remembering.

To summarize:

> 1. Not all items have the same chance of being stored in our memories.
> 2. Not all items that have been stored in our memories have the same chance of being recalled.
> 3. The attributes of the most available items, the ones having the highest chance of being recalled, are:
>   a. Well-known, familiar, and prominent items (due to either their general importance or personal relevance).
>   b. Items recently stored in memory.
>   c. Items we remember because they confirm our pre-existing beliefs.
>   d. Items that are vivid, dramatic, or emotional.
>
> Sampling from memory, then, is not random sampling but sampling according to availability. Hence, there is a considerable chance that samples created by memory are biased.

7.4 IS THE CHANCE OF ANY ITEM INDEPENDENT OF
THE CHANCE OF ANY OTHER?

The second requirement concerning the randomness of a sampling method is that any item's chances of being selected should be independent of the chance of any other item. In other words, after one particular item is selected, there should be no change in the other items' chances of being selected.

Does memory operate in this way? Studies of memory suggest that to an extent, human memory operates in the opposite way. We recall a fact or event because remembering something else triggered it ("that reminds me of . . . ."). Our memory often functions by way of associations. Recalling one item causes the recall of another, that is, the former decreases the recall chance of yet a third item, because it diverts our attention to a different thinking path.

If we return to the list of meaningful and meaningless words in the previous section and the samples we were able to recall from it, we will probably realize that in addition to recalling more meaningful words, those of us who recalled the word "cold" also recalled the word "warm" and vice versa. Usually, either both or neither were recalled. That is to say, recalling one of the two words increased the chance of recall for the second one.

Similarly, those of us who recalled from the list in the appendix a name of a famous actress (for instance, Elizabeth Taylor) very likely recalled another actress (Marilyn Monroe).

Again, therefore, sampling from memory does not follow the requirements of random sampling. The principle of associative recall, which determines to a considerable extent what we will recall next, constitutes a *contrast* to the principle that any item's chance of recall should be independent of the chances of other items.

A specific item's chances of being recalled are often dependent on the chances of other items. Therefore, sampling from memory is not random; there is a considerable chance that the recalled sample is a biased one.

If sampling from memory is not random, there is no advantage, of course, to sampling many items. The chances of the sample being representative are small.

Even in the ideal situation, which rarely if ever exists, in which sampling from memory is random, there is an additional drawback lowering the chances of the resulting sample being representative. Samples from memory are usually small in size, either because people do not remember much, or because they don't bother to take the time to recall many examples. *A small sample has few chances of being representative, even if it has been randomly selected.*

7.5 MEMORY CAPABILITIES—POSITIVE AND NEGATIVE ASPECTS

Because sampling from memory is not random, should we change our memory habits? That would be nearly impossible to do, for this is the way the human mind functions. Moreover, looking closely at these capabilities, we soon realize that even if we could change them (for example, to train ourselves to recall practically every item of a population) it would not be worthwhile. Memory is a valuable tool that serves us all our lives. We are constantly bombarded by vast quantities of information, far more than we can store and remember. Many things enter our minds (and our memories), but most of them fade away as if they did not exist at all. The human brain acts according to the "availability principle" for efficiency and convenience. We remember things that are important to us, things that are prominent and familiar. Insignificant things disappear from our memory.

—It is good that we forget insignificant details and remember important ones.

—It is good that we remember people we have met several times and forget those we saw only once.

—It is good that we recall things that have impressed us, no matter what the reasons, and forget the rest.

Imagine what would happen and how we would function if we remembered only a small and constant portion (according to our memory storage capacity) in a completely random way.

Our memory, as other human abilities, is a mechanism facilitating our functioning. In most cases, its capabilities enable us to function efficiently and adjust to our environment. Sometimes, however, they can mislead and fail us.

Thus, we should not modify our memory and its capabilities, but we ought to be aware of them in order to be able to evaluate the quality of "memory products." In this context, the products are "samples from memory."

Sampling from memory is not random, and therefore the resulting sample is usually unrepresentative. We ought to remember this and to view estimates and conclusions based on sampling from memory with appropriate skepticism and caution. We need to ask ourselves repeatedly: "Do I have any reason to suspect that my sample is biased?" Specifically, we should think in the following directions:

a. Was the sample drawn from the entire relevant population or from a sub-population that is unrepresentative of the total population? (What is the percentage, for instance, of people in your age group throughout the country who are regular church-goers? You definitely do not know all your peers in the whole country, and therefore you cannot sample from this huge group. You sample from your friends; are they representative of the entire population of people your age?)

b. Is it plausible that my sample is biased for the same reason? (Does the fact that I attend church affect the availability of other church-goers when I sample from memory?)

c. If it is plausible that the sample I chose is biased, can the direction of its bias be reconstructed? (Will church-goers tend to know and remember more church-goers?)

If we decide that our sample is biased, we will be justifiably less confident in the resulting estimate. If we are able to guess the direction of the bias, perhaps we will be able to correct our estimate. In any case, we should be cautious and thoroughly check samples produced from memory, because they are not selected randomly, but rather by availability.

Exercises for Sections 7.1–7.4

1. The following are several incorrect statements. Try to describe circumstances under which the principle of availability generated these statements.

Example.   Statement: The chances of being involved in a car accident at a particular crossroad is very high.

Possible circumstances: this was said by a worker in a gas station located at that crossroad who saw two accidents happen in the same week. Is this week representative of the whole year?

a. The percentage of smokers is steadily increasing.
b. All geniuses are somewhat mentally disturbed.
c. Three-quarters of young people finish high school.
d. Every fourth person is accused of some crime at least once in his or her life.
e. Relative to their number, female drivers are involved more often in car accidents than male drivers.
f. Each time I prepare really well for an exam, it gets cancelled.
g. The weather is usually nice on weekends.
h. Mishaps usually occur in threes.

i. There are more officials who treat the public in a highly negative way than officials who are exceptionally polite.

j. Buying large packages of any product is always more economical than buying smaller ones.

2. Several categories are written below, partly in code. For each one in turn, first decipher the code, then spend up to 30 seconds thinking of examples that fit the category. Write down all the examples you can think of, in the order you thought of them; then go on to the next category and repeat this procedure.

This is the code. Each letter in the code represents the letter immediately following it in the English alphabet. For instance, A in the code represents B, B represents C, K represents L, and so on; Z represents A.

People whose *kzrs mzld adfhmr* with S.
People who *vdzq fkzrrdr.*
Cities whose *onotkzshnm* is greater than *nmd lhkkhnm.*
Rszsdr smaller in size than *Nghn.*
Aqzmc names you would see in a *fqnbdqx* store.

Try to find in the samples you just produced examples demonstrating non-random sampling for any of the reasons discussed in this chapter. For example, for the last item, if you thought of Coke, did you also think of Pepsi because of the associative link between them?

3. How do advertising people utilize the availability phenomenon?

a. Find some printed ads demonstrating the use of availability.

b. Try to compose advertisement slogans (in rhymes if you like) that create a strong association between a particular objective and the product, so that whenever the object comes to mind, the product will be readily available.

Objective	*Product*
enjoying a soft drink	"TASTY DRINK"
the health of our teeth	"SNOW PUFF TOOTHPASTE"
good bicycles	"EASY RIDE" BICYCLES
a fashion pair of pants	"BODY" PANTS
a refreshing shower	"SCENT" SOAP
an enjoyable and healthy suntan	"SUN" SUNTAN LOTION
academic advancement	"WISDOM" ENCYCLOPEDIA

Appendix

1. Queen Elizabeth II
2. Billy Jean King
3. Sir John Gielgud
4. Susan B. Anthony
5. David Stockman
6. Christian Barnard
7. Jackie Onassis
8. Joe Hill
9. Henry Cabot Lodge
10. Dag Hammarskjöld
11. Archibald Cox
12. Elizabeth Taylor
13. Jack Kerouac
14. Marilyn Monroe
15. Henry Luce
16. George Harrison
17. Florence Nightingale
18. Ella Fitzgerald
19. Arthur Miller
20. Gloria Steinem
21. Leonard Bernstein
22. Cal Tjader
23. Soupy Sales
24. Indira Gandhi
25. George Bush
26. Pearl Buck
27. B. F. Skinner
28. Barbara Walters
29. Linda Ronstadt

III PROBABILITY ASSESSMENT

8 From Group Percentages to Individual Chances — Part I

8.1 INTRODUCTION

The following are excerpts from a fictitious radio interview with a space scientist and the manager of a weekly state lottery.

Interviewer (addressing the scientist): What are, in your opinion, the chances that we will succeed in making contact with intelligent creatures in outer space by the year 2000?

Scientist: I think the chances are pretty low, say 1 out of 100.

Interviewer: 1? 1 out of 100? How did you figure out that number?

Scientist: I considered all the scientific knowledge we have at present about outer space and also the technological advancements expected for the near future. In addition to that, I took into account that there are less than 20 years remaining before the year 2000, as well as other considerations I will not specify here. Viewing all these considerations together, I felt that my degree of belief is best expressed numerically as a 1% chance.

Interviewer: I understand that in your view, it's *unlikely* that we'll make some contact with intelligent creatures in outer space by 2000. Still, I do not completely understand your answer. Why do you say 1 chance in 100 rather than 5 or 10? How did you reach that particular number?

Scientist: To tell the truth, it is hard for me to explain precisely why I said 1 and not 5, for instance. My difficulty is not due to your or your listeners' possible lack of understanding of the scientific evidence I considered. It's just that I can't really specify the process I used to arrive at my answer; it wasn't an exact arithmetic computation involving addition, multiplication, or division of numbers. It was more like an educated intuition. The only thing I can say is that when I combined all the information at my disposal and considered the whole thing over and over again, I had a certain feeling that matches the number 1 out of 100 rather than 5 or 10 out of 100.[1]

Interviewer: If I had referred my question to one of your colleagues, do you think his or her inner feeling concerning this issue would be expressed by the same number?

Scientist: I have a colleague working closely with me. She shares the same information that I have, but most probably she would translate that information to different feelings about your question. I believe her reply would have been 10 out of 100.

Interviewer: Thank you very much indeed. (Turning to the lottery manager) Yesterday my wife bought a lottery ticket of yours. What would you say her chances of winning the grand prize are?

Lottery manager: I think she has some chance; for instance, a week ago a woman in Pittsburgh won that prize.

Interviewer: I know she has some chance, but can you tell me how high the chance is?

Lottery manager: Of course I can. This week exactly 800,000 tickets were sold. We offer many prizes, but only one ticket wins the grand prize each week. Hence the chances are 1 out of 800,000.

Interviewer: My wife's chance of winning the grand prize is, then, 1 out of 800,000?

Lottery manager: Yes, exactly.

If we check the answers of the two interviewees, we realize they reached their answers in different ways. The *scientist* considered the entire information at his disposal and thereafter a certain inner feeling evolved that he translated to a specific number. It is hard to describe in detail the process by which the scientist translated his considerations and knowledge to a feeling, and how that feeling was translated to a number. He emphasized the difficulty of describing this process in detail. He added that his colleague, who shares the same information concerning the subject under discussion, would have reached a larger number. In contrast, the *lottery manager* could produce the number she suggested quite easily by a *direct calculation* from the information available to her:

1. She knew how many tickets were sold (800,000).
2. She knew how many tickets the interviewer's wife bought (1 ticket).

---

[1]Note that the scientist is actually saying that he would have been indifferent had he been given the choice between these two gambles: (a) winning $1000 if some contact is established with creatures in outer space by the year 2000, versus (b) winning $1000 if the pointer in the chance circle lands on the shaded area, constituting 1% of the circle area (see Chapter 4).

3. She knew that only one ticket wins the grand prize.
4. She is familiar with the lottery method. This is a random method in which every ticket has exactly the same chance of winning.

From these four information items, the lottery manager drew the simple arithmetic conclusion concerning that chance: 1 out of 800,000.

There are cases in which obtaining a number from the information at our disposal is done in a *direct and obvious way accepted by everyone else.* In contrast, there are cases in which obtaining a number from available information is a matter of *personal feeling not necessarily shared by others.*

In the fourth chapter we dealt with cases of the second type. We presented the device of the chance wheel, which we used to help us in producing a number. We will return to similar cases later. This chapter and the next one deal exclusively with cases where the available information is used to produce the number in a direct, obvious, and accepted way. We will see the features of such cases and how translation of the information to a number expressing the chances can be done.

8.2 AN EXAMPLE

There are forty students in a particular class in law school, 30 men and 10 women. If you are asked to bet who will enter the classroom first next Monday morning, will you say "a man" or "a woman"? (Assume that you have no additional information concerning either the topic of the first Monday morning class or the habits of the women and men in that particular class.) A clever gambler will obviously bet on "a man," because there are more men than women in the class, and therefore the chances that the first entrant is a man are greater than that the first entrant is a woman.[2]

Let us recheck the data: There are 40 students in the class, 10 women and 30 men. Here is a new expression, "frequency"; its definition is as follows:

Frequency = number of cases (items) in the group

---

[2]Even if such a gambler loses the bet, because the first entrant happens to be a woman, nevertheless his or her decision is still clever. This is a situation of uncertainty and either result, the more expected as well as the less expected, can occur. In other words, a good decision can end in an undesired result.

Hence, the frequency of women in the class is 10 and the frequency of men is 30.

A smart gambler will bet on "a man" because the frequency of men in the group is greater than the frequency of women; thus, the chance of the first entrant being a man is greater than the chance of the first entrant being a woman.

To what extent, precisely, is the men's chance greater than the women's? If we wish to express these chances numerically, as percentages, within the range of 0 to 100, what numbers will we use? Obviously, the men's chance will be expressed by a number larger than 50, for the men have a greater chance than the women and these two are the only two possibilities.

There are 40 students in the class. A quarter of them (10 divided by 40) are women and three-quarters of them (30 divided by 40) are men. When these proportions are expressed as percentages, there are 25% women (a quarter multiplied by 100) and 75% men (three-quarters multiplied by 100). Together they make 100%.

A smart gambler will figure that the chances of the first entrant being a man is equal to the percentage of men in the class: 75%. And the chances that the first entrant will be a woman are 25%. There are three times as many men as women, and this ratio holds also for the chances: The chance that the first entrant will be a man is three times as great as the chance it will be a woman.

If we ask the same question about another class consisting of 42 students, 24 women and 18 men, the chance of the first entrant being a woman is about 57% ($\frac{24}{42} \times 100$), as is the women's percentage, and the chance it is a man is identical to the men's percentage, about 43% ($\frac{18}{42} \times 100$).

The chance of the first student entering the classroom being a man was determined *directly* by the class composition, the composition of the group under discussion. In the next section, we discuss the relationship between the chances for a single observation of a characteristic in question and the percentage of that characteristic in the group as a whole.

8.3 FROM GROUP PERCENTAGES TO INDIVIDUAL CHANCES

First, let us do a simple experiment. I have an ordinary thumbtack. What is the chance that if I drop it on the floor it will fall head down in contrast to falling on its side? If I drop it once, either one of these two results can occur; therefore, a single trial will not teach us anything about the relevant chance.

But suppose we throw the tack many times and calculate the percentage of trials on which it fell head down out of all the trials (number of throws). *If the tack shows more side falls than head-down falls, it will be possible to say that the chance of a side fall on a single throw is greater than the chance of a head-down fall.* Because these are the only two events possible, the chance of a side fall would then be higher than 50%. If the tack fell on its side about, say, 75% of the time in the trials, we could be even more accurate by saying that the chance of a side fall in a single throw is about 75%.

Such an experiment was carried out; a tack was thrown many times. Once in a while (after some throws) the results up to that point were recorded in the following manner:

a. Number of current throws (the first column in the table).

b. *Frequency* of head-down falls, namely, how many times up to that point the tack has fallen head down (the second column).

c. The *percentage* of times the tack fell head down out of the total number of throws to that point (the third column). This column was obtained by dividing column 2 by column 1 and multiplying by 100:

$$\frac{\text{column 2}}{\text{column 1}} \times 100 \text{ or } \frac{\text{the frequency of head-down falls}}{\text{total number of throws}} \times 100$$

The following is the table:

Column 1	Column 2	Column 3
Total Number of Throws	Frequency of Head Down Falls	Percentage of Head-Down Falls
1	1	$\frac{1}{1} \times 100 = 100$
2	1	$\frac{1}{2} \times 100 = 50$
5	2	$\frac{2}{5} \times 100 = 40$
10	3	$\frac{3}{10} \times 100 = 30$
30	8	$\frac{8}{30} \times 100 = 26.7$
50	14	$\frac{14}{50} \times 100 = 28$
100	30	$\frac{30}{100} \times 100 = 30$
200	80	$\frac{80}{200} \times 100 = 40$
300	118	$\frac{118}{300} \times 100 = 39.3$
400	160	$\frac{160}{400} \times 100 = 40$
500	202	$\frac{202}{500} \times 100 = 40.4$
600	241	$\frac{241}{600} \times 100 = 40.2$

Obviously, if you were to repeat the entire experiment, your table of results would be slightly different. For instance, the first throw could have resulted in a side fall rather than a head down fall, and then the percentage of head down falls in that throw would have been 0%.

Each line in the table is *one sample* of throws out of an infinite number of possible throws.

The third line shows the results of a sample of five throws. Two times the tack fell head down; the corresponding percentage is 40%. In the seventh line a sample of 100 throws is recorded, of which 30 were head down falls, for a percentage of 30%.

The total population we are interested in is the population of all possible throws of the thumbtack. Each line of the table is a *random* sample (see Section 6.6) from this population because: 1) each possible throw has an equal chance of inclusion in the sample; and 2) there is no connection whatsoever between any one throw and any other one.

We have learned that the chances of a random sample being representative increases as the size of the sample gets larger. Let us suppose that the tack has the same chance of either falling head down or on its side. Is it plausible to obtain, in a sample of 500 throws, 50 head down and 450 side falls? It is very unlikely. However, is it possible in a small sample, say 5 throws, to obtain four side falls and one head down fall? This result is much more likely.

We realize, therefore, that if we want to rely on the results of our tack throws in order to say something about the chances of it falling head down or on its side, it is worthwhile to have a large sample of throws. Such a sample has a much better chance than a small sample of representing the features of the tack falling.

This familiar effect is clearly demonstrated in the former table of results: in the small samples, the percentage of head down falls is highly inconsistent: 100%, 50%, 40%, 30%, and so on. As the sample size increases, the percentages stabilize: 39.3% (300 throws), 40% (400), 40.4% (500), and 40.2% (600).

If we continue the experiment and throw the tack 800 times and even more, we will realize that the percentage of head down falls stabilizes at around 40%. We can now say that the chances of the tack falling head down in *one* throw are approximately 40%, because this has been the percentage of head down falls in a large number of throws.

> We infer the chance of a specific outcome (e.g., head-down fall) in a single trial from the *percentage of that outcome* in a large number of trials (a large sample).

Another experiment demonstrating the same conclusion was conducted by a statistician named Räo. He put 10 balls into a sack; the balls were identical in shape and size but not in color: five were black, three were white, and two were red. The question was: what is the chance that a ball removed, at random, from the sack will be black? In order to answer this question, Räo, without looking in the sack, took out one ball, wrote down its color, and *returned it to the sack.* He then stirred the contents of the sack thoroughly. He repeated this procedure 1000 times (this is like throwing a tack 1000 times), and every once in a while recorded the following 3 data (like we did with the tack):

a. Number of balls taken out to this point (sample size)
b. How many of them were black (frequency of the outcome "black")
c. The percentage of black ball retrievals to this point (the percentage of the outcome "black").

When he finished the experiment, he realized that as the size of the sample (number of retrievals) became larger, the percentage of black balls stabilized at about 50%. Räo's conclusion was that the chance of retrieving one black ball from a sack containing 5 out of 10 balls is 50%.

Let us assume that we are asked to answer a similar question: "If I take out *one* ball from a sack having similar content of balls, what will be the color of the ball?" Obviously, we cannot answer this question with certainty. This is an uncertain situation, for three different outcomes (black, red, and white) are possible. Nevertheless, we can answer the question probabilistically:

a. We will prepare a set of exhaustive and mutually exclusive possibilities. The set is: black, red, and white. This set is *exhaustive,* for there are no other balls in the sack. The possibilities are mutually *exclusive* because no ball is painted with more than one color.

b. We will assign chances to the various possibilities. Räo's experiment has told us that the chance of a ball being black is 50% (because in 1000 retrievals the percentage of black balls stabilized at about 50%).

Had we also counted, at each point, the numbers and computed the percentages of white and red balls, we would have seen that the percentages tended to stabilize around 30% white and 20% red. Hence, the chance of a single ball being white is 30% and that of a single ball being red is 20%.

The chances that we will assign to the different possibilities are, then,

black	white	red	total[3]
50%	30%	20%	100%

---

[3]In a sample of 1000 retrievals, for instance, the percentages of black, red, and white balls should, obviously, add up to 100%. Similarly, this will be the case in any other sample. In a set of mutually exclusive and exhaustive possibilities, the degrees of belief based on sample information will add up to 100% across the various possibilities.

The sack contains a *group* of 10 items, identical in shape and size. The chance of any one item being sampled in one retrieval is equal to the chance of any other item, precisely because of this sameness in shape and size. Each one of the 10 balls has exactly the same chance.

We have seen that the chance of taking out a red ball, for example, is 20% (according to the percentage of red balls in many retrievals). We also know that there are 20% red balls in the sack. Is the identity of these numbers a coincidence? Is it only by accident that the percentage of red balls in many retrievals is identical to the percentage of red balls in the sack? No:

> The chance of retrieving a red ball (a chance that we figured out by computing the percentage of red balls in a large sample of retrievals) is exactly the same as the percentage of red balls in the sack—20%.
>
> The chance of taking out a black ball (a chance that we found out by computing the percentage of black balls in a large sample of retrievals) is exactly the same as the percentage of black balls in the sack—50%. This rule applies also to the white balls.

This lawfulness exists only if all the balls are identical in shape and size, for only then does each ball have the same chance of being sampled. If, for instance, the red balls were bigger than the other balls, then in every sampling, their chances of being picked would be greater, and in a larger sample (say 1000) there would have been more than 20% red balls, their percentage in the sack. But if all balls have the same chance of being sampled, the percentage of a certain color in a large sample is equal (approximately) to the percentage of this color among all the balls. Furthermore, we previously inferred the chances of drawing just one ball of a given color from the percentage of balls of that color in the sack.

We can formulate all this as a more general rule:

> If all items in a group have the same chance of being sampled, then the *percentage of a specific characteristic in a large sample* is equal to the *percentage of this characteristic among all items in the group*. This percentage is also equal to the *chances that the specified characteristic will be the outcome* when only *one* item is sampled.

Let us review the former examples:

—It is clear now why in a class consisting of 30 men and 10 women the chance that the first student entering the classroom will be a man is 75%:

1. Let us assume that every morning, each one of the students has the same chance of being the first to enter the classroom.

2. If we had checked who was the first to enter every morning for a long period of time, we would have found that for about 75% of the mornings it was a man. This is because men comprise 75% of the class.

3. This percentage is also the chance that we will assign to any single morning in connection with the question under discussion. We will say that there is a 75% chance of a man being the first to enter the classroom.

—It is also clear now why the chance of the woman winning the grand prize is 1 out of 800,000:

There are 800,000 tickets (like 10 balls in a sack), only one of which will be the winner (like 5 black balls). What is the chance that the woman who bought a single ticket is holding the winning one (like the chance that in a single retrieval we will pick out a black ball)? The chance in percentage terms is:

$$\frac{1}{800,000} \times 100 = \frac{1}{8,000}\% = 0.000125\%.$$

What is, then, the common denominator of all three problems?

—The chance of picking out a black ball (balls in a sack)?
—The chance that the first student entering the classroom is a man?
—The chance of winning the grand prize (lottery)?

1. In all these problems there is a *defined group* having a given size (*10* balls in a sack, *40* students in a class, and *800,000* lottery tickets sold in a given week).

2. A question is asked concerning the chance of a *single specific characteristic* or *result* (a *black* ball, a *male* student, a *winning* ticket).

3. If we sample randomly one item of the group, then each item in the group has the same chance of being selected (each ball, each student, or each ticket has the same chance).

4. In order to compute the chance in all three cases, we check:

    a. *the size of the specific group* (10, 40, 800,000 for the ball, classroom, and lottery questions, respectively).

    b. *the size of the subgroup* having the relevant characteristic (5, 30, 1), and

   c. *the percentage of the subgroup* in the entire group (50%, 75%, 0.000125%).
This percentage is the chance we assign to the question concerning the chance of a single item having the relevant characteristic.

When I was visiting my family in the Midwest, I met a young man, George, who is a student at Midwest University. Later, my family and I had a vigorous discussion about the use of marijuana on U.S. college campuses, and I began to wonder whether George, the young man I met, smoked marijuana.

I could not answer that question conclusively; indeed, I knew very little about George, having met him only briefly. But I wondered about the chances that he is a dope smoker. How could I compute those chances accurately?

I ought to define both the appropriate group and the relevant characteristic. Here the appropriate group is:
—All male students enrolled at Midwest University.
Defining the relevant characteristic requires a little more care; what exactly do I mean by "dope smoker"? Remember, I must satisfy the clairvoyance test in this definition. My family and I decided after some discussion that "dope smoker" meant:
   —A person who has smoked or otherwise ingested marijuana at least once every two weeks for the last six months.
The relevant characteristic is then:
   —A male student enrolled at Midwest U. who is a dope smoker.

Note that the relevant characteristic is always defined as a *subgroup* of the appropriate group.

Now that our group and subgroup are carefully defined, we need only obtain the appropriate data in order to calculate the percentage:

$$\frac{\text{Number of male MU students who smoke dope}}{\text{Number of male students at MU}} \times 100.$$

I will use this percentage to express my belief that George, about whom I know nothing else, smokes dope.

When we have the relevant data, it is simple to compute the chances. However, in most interesting and important cases, there are no available data either on the size of the group or on the size of the relevant subgroup. In such cases, we will use estimates. Sometimes we will directly estimate the percentage and in other instances we will estimate the size of each group and thus obtain the desirable percentage. The next chapter will discuss these estimation procedures.

Exercises for Chapter 8

1. What are the chances that the next person you meet was born:
   a. On a Saturday?
   b. On the Fourth of July?
   c. On Christmas day?

2. What are the chances that this same person is a twin? What information do you need to answer this question?

3. Take a paper clip and bend the center part out slightly, just far enough so that it is possible for the paper clip, when tossed, to land resting sideways. Now toss the paper clip 300 times and record, for each toss, whether the center (smaller) part landed *up, down,* or *sideways.* From these data, construct a table like the thumb-tack table in this chapter. Because you are dealing here with three outcomes rather than two, you will have to expand Column 2 to three columns: Frequency Up, Frequency Down, and Frequency Sideways. What are the chances that, on the next toss, the paper clip will land with the center part up?

4. Below are two tables giving frequency data. From them, formulate two questions in terms of chances ("What are the chances that...?"). Answer each of your questions by:
   a. Defining a total group
   b. Defining the relevant characteristic
   c. Defining the subgroup that has that characteristic
   d. Calculating the percentage that the subgroup is within the total group.

Women in the Armed Services, 1978

Total military	2,062,000
Women	134,000
Officers, total	274,000
Women officers	17,000
Enlisted personnel	1,788,000
Enlisted women	117,000

Total Arrests, by Age Group, 1978

under 15	728,198
15–24	4,808,664
25–34	2,111,396
35–44	1,036,863
45–54	669,074
55 or older	411,998
not known	8,898
total	9,775,091

9 From Group Percentages to Individual Chances — Part II

9.1 THE USE OF ESTIMATES FOR COMPUTING CHANCES

—Tonight I am going to the theater. I have just discovered that my friend, Ralph, has also bought a ticket for the show tonight. My seat is in the 15th row. What is the chance that Ralph will sit in the same row?

In the previous chapter, it was shown that we can make inferences about such chances from the percentage of the number of seats in row 15 (except mine) out of the total number of seats in the theater (except mine). This is the procedure:

a. Define the entire group: total number of seats in the theater, not counting mine.
b. Define the subgroup: number of seats in row 15, not counting mine.
c. Find the size of these two groups.
d. Compute the appropriate percentage:

$$\frac{\text{number of seats in row 15, minus one}}{\text{total number of seats in the theater, minus one}} \times 100$$

This percentage is the chance that Ralph will sit in the same row that I do, provided, of course, that I am willing to assume that Ralph's ticket is equally likely to be for any seat in the theater except mine.

Even with simple problems like this one, we usually do not have accurate data on the size of each group; this is even more often the case with more complicated and interesting problems. For instance, the chance of recovering from a specific disease (what is the usual percentage of people recovering from it?); the chance of my friend giving birth to twins (what is the percentage of twin births out of all births?); my chance of being accepted to the Navy school for combat pilots (what is the percentage of people accepted to the school out of all applicants?).

In such cases, in which the relevant information is lacking, we will use an already familiar method—estimation. Three estimation procedures are available:

A. Estimating the Size of Each Group

—We will attempt to estimate the total number of seats in the theater. There are, for example, about 30 rows in the theater's main hall and 30 more in the balcony. By estimating the number of seats in rows located in various areas in the main hall and balcony, we reached a total estimation figure of 3000, approximately.

—Estimating the number of seats in row 15, we figured out there are about 50.

The chance, then, that Ralph will sit in the same row that I do is:

$$\frac{50}{3,000} \times 100 = 1.6\%$$

(Subtracting 1, my seat, from both 50 and 3000 is not significant, since these figures are esimates rather than the true values.)

Returning to the problem that ended the last chapter, how can we evaluate the chances that George smokes dope? Probably we do not have accurate information concerning the size of each of the relevant groups. Instead, we will use estimates:

1. Define the total group: male students enrolled at Midwest University.
2. Define the subgroup: male students enrolled at MU who smoke dope.
3. Estimate the size of each group.
4. Compute the percentage: $\frac{\text{size estimate of the subgroup}}{\text{size estimate of the total group}} \times 100$.

Sometimes it will be difficult for us to estimate the size of one or both groups. In such cases, we will use a different method in order to obtain the desired percentage.

B. Estimation Based on Samples

In this method, we *estimate the desired percentages in a sample,* rather than in the entire group. For instance, "I know about 20 male students at MU. Four of them use dope. Thus, the percentage of dope smokers is approximately 20% ($\frac{4}{20} \times 100$)." This method is convenient when we have no idea about the size of one or both groups but we can recall enough examples to create a sample upon which we will base our estimates. Such a sample is, obviously, as vulnerable as any other one: Are the students I know from MU representative of all male students at MU? Isn't the number of my student acquaintances too small to constitute a decent sample?

In the two estimation methods discussed, we *compute* the percentage, either relying on estimates of the sizes of both groups, or relying on relevant samples. There is another estimation method in which the percentage we seek is itself estimated.

C. Direct Estimation of the Percentage

Very often we estimate the percentage directly rather than computing it from estimates of groups or samples. "I have read in the newspaper that 37% of all college males smoke dope. But MU is a rather conservative university compared to, say, California colleges. Therefore, I estimate the desired percentage as being about 25%."

In this case, the problem is not decomposed so that we deal with its elements, the appropriate two groups. Instead, we estimate the percentage *directly* utilizing some information we possess. We should keep in mind, though, that this is an estimate just like any other. We might be wrong in remembering what the newspaper said, or in correcting that estimate on the basis of our knowledge of a particular university.

To summarize:

We can use one of the following three methods in order to obtain estimates of chances:

a. Estimate both the size of the relevant total group and that of the subgroup; then compute the percentage utilizing both estimates and from it infer the desired chance.

b. Carry out the same procedure using a sample of the total group: Obtain estimates or exact figures of the sample size and of the number of items having the relevant characteristic *in the sample;* then compute the percentage, which is also the chance, using the sample estimates.

c. Estimate the percentage (the chance) directly using some information available to you.

As with other numerical estimates, it is a good idea to use more than one estimation technique whenever possible. When two different estimation techniques produce greatly different estimates of the chances, this signals possible errors (see Section 5.6).

9.2 WHAT IS THE RELEVANT TOTAL GROUP?

In the examples we have discussed so far, we did not have great difficulty in defining the appropriate groups. Sometimes, however, it is not completely clear exactly what group we are trying to estimate. For example:
—My friend gave birth last year. What are the chances that she gave birth to twins?[1]
—My friend is pregnant and due to give birth next month. What are the chances she will have twins?

In these two examples the appropriate total group is "all births" and the subgroup is "twin births." Here we have two problems:

Problem 1. "All births" since when? This a huge group. How could we count all births up to now in order to compute the percentage of twin births out of them? We can overcome this problem by using a really large sample, say, all U.S. births in the last decade.

Problem 2. In the first example, my friend has already given birth. Thus, the event really is an item from the defined group, "all births in the last decade." In contrast, the second example involves a birth that has not yet occurred. The event is not really a member of the group we are using to compute the chances, for the group is of births in the past, whereas the event is in the future.

We encounter this problem whenever we use past data to assess the chances of future events (aren't these often the most interesting issues?). In so doing, we assume that the similarity between the past cases and the future case justifies our inferences from the past to the future.

A friend of mine has a son who will enter Midwest University next year. What are the chances that he will, while in college, be a dope smoker? We will answer this question as we have answered the question concerning George, who is now attending MU. When we do, we are assuming that the situation in the future in this respect (the rate of dope smoking at MU) is not going to change significantly.

What is the chance of at least one snowy day in Atlanta next February? If we believe next year to be basically similar to previous years (as far as winter

---

[1] Let us assume that we do not know whether or not she has given birth to twins in the past.

weather is concerned), we will use as a group several February months of the past and we will check the percentage of those February months in which there was at least one snowy day. While discussing the topic of estimation in Chapter 6, we said that to the extent that the sample is large, the chance of it being representative increases. Hence, in attempting to estimate chances of future events, like at least one snowy day next February in Atlanta, we would do well to base the estimate on a sample of many past years, as many as 100. Is this always the case?

—What is the chance that my friend, who is moving to an apartment in mid-town Manhattan, will experience a burglary during her first year there? If we check back on the burglary statistics for the past 100 years, we will find that over time burglaries have substantially increased in mid-Manhattan. The 1930s for instance, are not at all representative of the present (nor of the future) in this respect. It is better, then, to base our estimation on a much smaller sample of recent years, say, the last five years; these years are more representative of the present and of our expectations for the future.

To summarize:

If the relevant total group is too large, it will suffice to use a sample for estimating the chances, providing that it is plausible to assume that this sample is representative of the total group.

When assigning chances to a future event, the estimates can be based on similar past cases, providing that it is reasonable to assume that no substantial change has occurred or will occur with regard to the characteristic whose chances we are estimating.

Exercises for 9.1 and 9.2

1. The following are questions involving chances of various events. For each question, do the following:

    a. Specify the total group and the subgroup having the relevant characteristic.
    b. Find samples representative of these groups (consult friends if you need to).
    c. Estimate the sizes of the samples you chose.
    d. Compute the chance of the event in question by using the figures you obtained in step c.

An example.   What is the chance that the next ring of my telephone will turn out to be a wrong number?

    a. Total group: Incoming phone calls to my house in the past and future. Subgroup: Wrong number calls.

    b. Sample of the group: Number of calls last week. Sample of the subgroup: Number of wrong numbers last week.

    c. I get approximately 6 calls daily during the week and about 20 on the weekends, which makes about 50 incoming calls weekly. Last week, as far as I remember, there were two wrong numbers.

    d. The chance, then, is: $\frac{2}{50} \times 100 = 4\%$.

Here are the questions. *What is the chance of*:

1. Finding at least one typographical error on the third page of tomorrow's local newspaper?
2. Running out of gas sometime next month?
3. Finding a coin on the sidewalk during a 1 hour walk in town?
4. Being contacted at least once by a pollster during the coming year?

9.3 REDUCING THE GROUP

William Smith, a high ranking official of the Pentagon, invited Jean Baker, a Pentagon security officer, to lunch. Following is their conversation over lunch:

Smith: Yesterday at a concert I met a Russian named Boris Yermilov. He works in the Soviet consulate. Do you know him?

Baker: No.

Smith: We talked during the intermission and he invited me to a dinner at his house next week.

Baker: You don't mean you...

Smith: That is precisely why I wanted to talk to you. You have more experience and knowledge concerning Russian diplomats than I do. What is, in your opinion, the chance Yermilov is an undercover Soviet intelligence agent?

Baker: I do not know Yermilov and you did not tell me anything about him, except that he is an employee of the Soviet consulate here. Based on my experience of recent years, I would say that about 60% of the personnel at the Soviet consulate are actually undercover agents, whose official positions are secondary to their intelligence gathering functions. Thus, I would estimate the chance that Yermilov is such an agent as about 60%.

Here, as in the former examples, the assessor has relied upon the percentage of similar cases in the group, namely, the percentage of those who are believed to be undercover agents, out of all Soviet consulate staff members. Let us proceed with the conversation:

Smith: I do know something about Yermilov that may change the picture a little. He works in the economic delegation at the consulate.

Baker: Oh, that's different. In my opinion, the percentage of Soviet spys among Soviet consulate economists is much less than among the others. I would estimate it as perhaps 25%. Therefore, the chances that Yermilov is a spy has decreased to 25%.

We have seen that Smith furnished Baker with another information item concerning Yermilov, and that she had to define a new total group from which to estimate the appropriate percentage. That is, we are no longer dealing with the percentage of undercover spys among all Soviet consulate staff members in Washington, D.C. in recent years, but rather among all economic delegation personnel. This additional information item was inserted into the redefinition of the groups in the following manner.

Total group.   All staff members of the economic delegation in the Soviet consulate in Washington, D.C.

Subgroup.   All staff members of the economic delegation in the Soviet consulate in Washington, D.C. who are also Soviet undercover intelligence agents.

Thus, the two groups are reduced. The percentage can either increase, decrease, or remain the same (in the present case, it has decreased).

If William Smith had also told Jean Baker that Yermilov flys at least once a month to the Soviet Union, she should have considered two even smaller groups.

Total group.   All staff members of the economic delegation in the Soviet consulate in Washington, D.C. who fly at least once a month to the USSR.

Subgroup.   All staff members of the economic delegation in the Soviet consulate in Washington, D.C. who fly at least once a month to the USSR and who are also Soviet underground intelligence agents.

The chance that Yermilov is an undercover agent is the percentage of the subgroup within this newly reduced total group.

From the following diagram, count or compute each of the following:

(a) The total number of Soviet consulate staff members.
(b) The number of Soviet consulate staff members who are also undercover agents.
(c) The percentage of agents among all Soviet consulate personnel.
(d) The total number of economic delegation members.

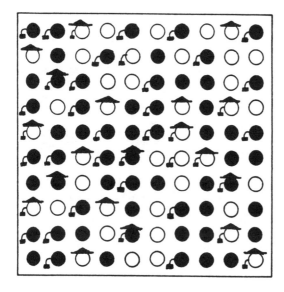

○ Soviet Consulate Member
● Undercover Intelligence
⛑ Economic Delegation Member
✊ Visits USSR At Least Once A Month

(e) The number of economic delegation members who are also under-cover spys.
(f) The percentage of agents in the Soviet economic delegation.
(g) The number of economic delegation members who fly to the USSR at least once a month.
(h) The number of economic delegation members who fly to the USSR at least once a month and are also intelligence agents.
(i) The percentage of agents out of all Soviet economic delegation members who fly to the USSR at least once a month.

With each additional piece of information, the total group gets smaller (*a* vs. *d* vs. *g*) and the percentage of intelligence agents in the group changes (*c* vs. *f* vs. *i*).[2] The change in the percentage indicates that the additional items of information, "he is in the economic delegation" and "he flies to the USSR at least once a month," are relevant.

---

[2] From 60% to 25% to 33%.

> It is worthwhile to use additional information to re-define the groups involved. Each additional item of information diminishes the size of both the total group and the subgroup; it may also modify the estimated chances significantly.

9.4 THE RELEVANCE OR DIAGNOSTICITY OF AVAILABLE INFORMATION

Is it useful to take into account *each* piece of information available to us? Should we consider, for instance, the fact that Yermilov is completely bald-headed? Let us define the appropriate groups accordingly:

—The total number of economic delegation staff members in the Washington, D.C. Soviet consulate who fly to the Soviet Union at least once a month and who have bald heads.

—The total number of economic delegation staff members in the Washington, D.C. Soviet consulate who fly to the Soviet Union at least once a month, who have bald heads, and who are undercover intelligence agents.

The size of each of these groups is obviously smaller than the former groups, in which the information about baldness was not used.

Will the percentage (the ratio between both groups multiplied by 100), from which we infer the chance of being a spy, always change when new information is used? No; it is always possible that the ratio will remain the same although the size of the groups change. A change in the percentage will indicate that the new item of information is relevant, but it is a retrospective indicator, because the item has already been taken into account. We would like to check the relevancy of each additional item *in advance,* in order to decide whether to use it.

To check relevance, one has to ask oneself whether it is reasonable to assume that the percentage of agents out of those who have bald heads is different from the percentage of those who do not have bald heads. As there is no reason to assume that baldness can be regarded as a relevant item of information, it should not be taken into account.

A check, in advance, of an item like "flies to the USSR at least once a month" should be done by asking oneself whether the percentage of agents out of those who fly frequently is different from the percentage of agents who do not. This time the answer will probably be positive and this item would be taken into account (as we did).

Information about a person's position (high vs. low rank), travel abroad (travel much vs. little), and education (elementary school, high school, higher education) is relevant if one believes that the percentage of under-cover agents differs with the different values each of these items can take.

When we conclude that taking a certain item of information into account will not change the percentage, we will regard this item as *irrelevant* or *non-diagnostic information*. If we believe that consideration of a certain item will *change* the percentage, we will consider it as *relevant* or *diagnostic information*.

Irrelevant information does not change the estimate and therefore is not beneficial. However, can it be harmful? Sometimes it can lessen the quality of the estimate. Let us assume, for example, that among the staff members of the Soviet economic delegation in Washington, D.C. in recent years there were only two people who shared the following two characteristics: travel-ling quite often to their homeland and being bald-headed. Later it turned out that one of them was an undercover intelligence agent. Would it be reasonable to say that Yermilov's chance of being a spy is 50%, just because there were two Soviets similar to him in these respects and one of them was a spy? The additional information (being bald) excessively reduced the size of the relevant groups so that the total group is now made up of only two people. This is a rather small sample, and, as you may recall, small samples have serious drawbacks.

In addition, in many cases we do not have accurate information about the sample sizes; instead, we are thinking about the relevant groups, trying to estimate their sizes. It is far more difficult to think about such small groups that are multiply-specified. When we search our memory, we may obtain highly biased estimates.

It is better, then, to ignore, in our example, the baldness information and rely on information concerning "economists flying frequently to the USSR." These characteristics will lead to forming a large enough group that the estimate obtained from it is reasonably reliable.

In summary, we were faced with the dilemma of attempting to consider every piece of information; doing so may improve the estimate by defining a more appropriate group, but, at the same time, considering all information may lead us to a group so small that the estimate is unreliable. We recom-mend, therefore, that every available item of information be checked for relevance. If an item seems relevant, we would include it in defining the groups (even though we are thus decreasing their size); any irrelevant items should be disregarded, to avoid the unnecessary reduction of the sizes of the groups.

Sometimes, however, we have so much information that even after disregarding the irrelevant pieces, the samples are too small or difficult to think about. What should we do in such cases? The following is a discussion of such situations.

9.5 EXCEPTIONAL PROBLEMS

Suppose I learn more about George, the student at Midwest University. He is now a junior, majoring in Electrical Engineering, with a cumulative grade point average of 3.2. He grew up in a small Kansas town (population 4100) and was the valedictorian of his high school class. At the University he is an avid fan of rock music and frequently attends rock concerts. What are the chances that George smokes dope?

All the information items concerning George appear relevant. Some of them will increase and others decrease the chances that he smokes dope. For example, the fact that George grew up in a small town in Kansas may decrease that chance; on the other hand, the fact that he often goes to rock concerts may increase it.

Trying to estimate the chances, we define the groups:

Total group.   Male students at Midwest University who are juniors in Electrical Engineering with GPA's of 3.2 who grew up in a small town in Kansas, were validictorians in high school, and who now frequently attend rock concerts.

Subgroup.   Dope smokers among the group defined above.

It is likely that even if we had full information on every Midwest University student we would not find even one other, besides George, who has these same characteristics. We just could not form a group.

Such cases are called *exceptional problems* because it is difficult—sometimes impossible—to form a group of similar cases.

An exceptional problem is one for which we have plenty of relevant information; therefore, it is hard to find many cases similar to the discussed one in order to form a group.

In Chapters 8 and 9, we demonstrated computation of chances according to *frequencies,* relying on the percentage of similar cases in the appropriate group. The requirement for applying such an approach is the ability to find a large enough group. When such a group can be found, relative frequencies determine our degree of confidence.

Elsewhere in the book we have presented exceptional problems. For example, at the end of Chapter 4 we asked you to assess the probability that Reagan will be reelected in 1984. We assume that you have a lot of knowledge about Reagan that is relevant; you will quickly realize that no previous president is similar in all respects to Reagan. Because an appropriate group cannot be found, one cannot entirely rely on frequentistic methods to arrive at any assessment of chances.

Consider, as we did in Chapter 4, an intelligence officer who is assessing the chances of war. Had he done so by relying solely on frequencies, he should have done the following:

a. Analyze the current situation and check the relevancy of the available information.
b. Search in the past for identical periods (times during which the military and political situation was the same as now).
c. Check the percentage of these periods that actually led to war.

Such a procedure is ridiculous; past situations are rarely, if ever, identical in all characteristics to the present situation. The intelligence officer will never be able to get to step *c*.

> Methods of estimating chances that rely exclusively on frequency counts can only be used when a relatively large group of similar cases is available.

Exercises for Sections 9.4 and 9.5

The following are questions involving chances of various events. For each question:

a. Specify the total group and subgroup having the relevant characteristics.
b. List an item of information that appears to be relevant (that is, one that will alter the chances).
c. List one information item that seems irrelevant.
d. If the question seems to deal with an exceptional problem, point that out and elaborate.

An Example:

What are the chances that at least one time during the coming week when I leave my house, I will meet friends coming to visit me?

a. Total group: All the times that I have left my house in the last year. Subgroup: All the times that, while leaving my house, I have met friends coming to visit me, during the past year.

b. Relevant information: The number of my friends who have told me they plan to visit me this coming week.

c. Irrelevant information: My house is painted white.

These are the questions: *What are the chances that*:

1. The bullet I am about to shoot will hit the target accurately?
2. The next person to go on trial for murder in my state will be found guilty?
3. My child will be more than 5 ft. 8 in. tall when the child is 18 years old?
4. Human kind will make contact with intelligent creatures in outer space within the next 10 years?
5. The bridge will collapse while we are crossing it?

10 Estimating Chances in Exceptional Problems

10.1 INTRODUCTION

We will start with several examples.

Example 1. Dan is a high school senior. He is an attractive young man, above average in height. He has excellent grades, not because he is brilliant, but because he is bright and works hard at his studies. He is a well-rounded and well-liked student who plays on the tennis team and who was elected treasurer of the senior class. While sociable, he has not dated as often as many of his peers, although he does have a girl friend this year. For many years he has wanted to become a physician, and he plans to go to college as a pre-med student.

What is Dan's chance of being accepted into a medical school?

Example 2. Dick is a tall, handsome junior in one of the best high schools in town. During his sophomore year, he was a good student. But recently, his grades and behavior have deteriorated. He often quarrels with his peers and spends time with a bad crowd. He drinks a lot of beer and it is also rumored that he takes amphetamines ("speed"). Several times he has disappeared for several days. He is surly with his parents and refuses to tell them where he has been. Discussing Dick's case with the school's psychologist, the principal tried to estimate Dick's *chance of becoming entangled with the law* (becoming entangled with the law will be defined here as: a police file concerning Dick will be opened within two years).

Example 3. Judy is a beautiful young woman. She takes care of herself and her figure is slim and sexy. She always wears fashionable clothes and is frequently seen in beauty parlors, coffee houses, and clothing boutiques. *What is the chance that Judy is a fashion model?*

Example 4.   Robert is a young writer and journalist teaching part-time in one of the universities on the East coast. His students regard him as a sensitive, honest, and interesting person. He is now spending most of his time writing his second book, which is about three young men in the Vietnam war. Robert's first book received enthusiastic reviews by literary critics.

What is the chance his second book will fail (that is, will sell less than 1000 copies a year)?

What is common to all these examples? Using the terminology of the former chapter, these are all exceptional problems having a multitude of detail; for each, therefore, it is hard to find appropriate groups of similar cases. It is hard to find many people whose description and history completely match the person portrayed in each of the four examples. For instance, it will be extremely difficult to find other books that deal with three young men in Vietnam that are also the second book of a young writer and journalist who is an instructor at a university.

The detailed information creates a picture of living human beings, each one having a history and personality of his or her own. Thus it is difficult in each case to find "duplicates" and organize them in a group. This problem becomes even more severe when more personal aspects enter the picture. Let us assume that it is Dan's mother who is estimating his chance of being accepted to a medical school. She knows "her Dan" better, having an enormous amount of details about him. She conceptualizes Dan as a very special and unique person. In addition, Dan's mother has certain aspirations concerning her son and it is not easy for her to ignore all these when estimating his chances of being accepted into medical school.

With all these problems, we cannot use the *frequentistic approach*. We cannot compute the percentage of people or items having the same characteristic out of the relevant total group.

What should we do with such problems? Before attempting to answer this question, we will show a common approach to estimating chances when considering exceptional problems. Later we will discuss the possible contribution of the frequentistic approach even to such problems.

10.2 THE COMMON APPROACH—HOW DO WE USUALLY ESTIMATE CHANCES OF EXCEPTIONAL PROBLEMS?

Let us review the examples presented in the beginning of this chapter:

You probably assigned Dan a high chance of being accepted in medical school on the grounds that:

—Dan has traits that are necesary to be a doctor.

—Dan is an ideal candidate.

—Most doctors were like Dan in high school.

And what did you think about Judy?

—She looks and acts like a fashion model.

—Most fashion models look like Judy.

What about Robert? The chances his second book will fail seem small because:

—Robert looks like a "symbol of success."

—He is a sensitive and promising young writer.

—Robert's first book was a success. Why should the second one fail?

Such arguments can teach us something about our way of thinking. We can divide them into two groups:

1. Reasoning *based on the similarity between a description and a prototype.* We find (or, sometimes, fail to find) a striking similarity between the *described case* and the *characteristic* that we are attempting to estimate: Dick is acting like a *typical* pre-delinquent. Judy looks like a fashion model ought to look. But Robert is just not the usual "failure" as a writer.

2. *Frequentistic reasoning.*

—"Most doctors were like Dan in high school."

—"Most fashion models look like Judy."

We will see in a moment that such reasoning leads us to faulty conclusions.

Similarity between a description and a prototype. Let us look again at Judy's description (Example 3). What are the chances that she is: An airline stewardess? An owner or employee of a boutique? An actress? A cosmetics salesperson? A television announcer? Rich and unemployed?

We will try now to answer these questions in an orderly way as we recommended doing in Chapter 3, where we discussed the methods of counting all possibilities. Doing as recommended there, we will write down all of Judy's possible professions and organize them in a list of exhaustive and exclusive possibilities. Then we need to divide our 100% confidence among all possibilities (see Chapter 4).

Doing so, we realize immediately that it is exaggerated to assign, say, 70% for "fashion model" because it leaves only 30% chance to spread across all other occupations. The problem here is that similarity considerations do not comply with the rules concerning chance. When we assign chances to mutually exclusive and exhaustive events, our assignment is compensatory: the more confidence we assign to one possibility, the less we have available to assign to all the other possibilities. Out total store of confidence is a constant, that is, the chances must add up to 100%. But similarity does not work this way. There is no constant store of similarity, so our assessments of similarity need not be compensatory. Judy can be highly similar to an airline stewardess *and* highly similar to a fashion model *and* highly similar to a boutique owner, and so on. But with chances we are limited to 100%. So, if the chance of her being a stewardess is high, then the chances of her having other occupations must be small.

Thus, similarity between a description and a prototype is *not* a good basis for assessing chances; it is likely to mislead, sometimes leading to ridiculous conclusions.

Frequentistic considerations. What is wrong with applying the frequentistic approach, namely, using the reasoning: "Most fashion models look like Judy"?

It is advantageous to utilize the frequentistic approach, *but only if it is applied properly,* that is, using correct definitions of the total group and the subgroup. In Judy's case, the total group is "all young women who resemble Judy in all details mentioned." The subgroup is "the fashion models out of the total group." Therefore, the *correct frequentistic consideration* should be: *"the percentage of fashion models out of those young women who resemble Judy."*

Compare these groups with the total group and the subgroup underlying the reasoning "most fashion models look like Judy." The total group is "all fashion models." The subgroup is "the group of young women who resemble Judy." Thus, the *mistaken frequentistic consideration* is *"the percentage of young women resembling Judy out of all fashion models"* (i.e., "most fashion models look like Judy").

It is easy to show that one should not make inferences about one of these frequentistic arguments based on the other one. If it is true that "most fashion models look like Judy" (the mistaken reasoning), it is not necessarily true that "most young women who look like Judy are fashion models" (the correct reasoning). In the same way, if it is true that most heroin addicts drank milk as children, it does not logically follow that most people who drank milk as children become heroin addicts.

Consider Fig. 10.1. The large rectangle represents young women who resemble Judy. The smaller areas represent those who hold the jobs Judy might hold: fashion model, stewardess, actress. The shaded area represents fashion models. Of these, most resemble Judy (shown by cross-hatching). But among all the young women who look like Judy, only about 1/6 (approximately 17%) are fashion models. In other words, only 17% out of all young women who look like Judy are actually fashion models. When we are asked to estimate the chance of Judy being a fashion model, we are asked to estimate "the percentage of fashion models among those young women who look like her." Based on the information given in Fig. 10.1, the correct answer to this question should have been 17%, approximately.

The information, "Most fashion models look like Judy" is not irrelevant to the question, "What are the chances that Judy is a fashion model?" But the relationship between the two is complex. One *cannot* infer directly from the percentage of A in B to the percentage of B in A. When using a frequentistic approach, it is essential that one carefully and properly define the relevant groups and make sure that the estimate is based on the ratio between the correct two groups.

When estimating chances, we tend to rely heavily on:
   a. similarity between descriptions and prototypes,
   b. mistaken frequentistic considerations.
Instead we ought to:
   a. avoid the errors similarity considerations can
      induce by listing a mutually exclusive and
      exhaustive set of possibilities.
   b. check whether the group and subgroup we use for
      frequency estimates are indeed the correct ones.

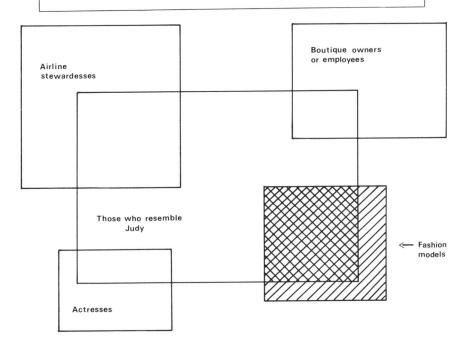

FIG. 10.1   A Diagram of the Fashion Model Example.

10.3 THE DESIRABLE APPROACH—HOW TO APPLY FREQUENTISTIC CONSIDERATIONS WITH EXCEPTIONAL PROBLEMS

Frequentistic Reasoning for a Preliminary Estimate

Although it is often difficult to find other cases similar to an exceptional case (and when we do find them, there are usually too few of them to rely on for our estimates), we do not have to refrain completely from using frequentistic considerations. Instead of relying on frequencies as the sole source of our estimate, we use them for a starting point. Let us take another look at Dick's case (Example 2). What do we know about him?

- a. He is a junior in a good high school in town.
- b. He was a good student last year.
- c. His academic performance has deteriorated.
- d. He attends school only irregularly and has disappeared for days at a time.
- e. He quarrels with fellow students.
- f. He drinks a lot of beer.
- g. It is also said about him that he uses amphetamines.
- h. He hangs out with a bad crowd.
- i. He is surly and withdrawn from his parents.

What is Dick's chance of "becoming entangled" with the law (i.e., a police file concerning him will be opened within two years)? Having all this information about Dick, we are tempted to say that the chances are quite high, since:

—"This is the image of an early delinquent."

—"Most delinquents started doing similar things."

But these considerations reflect the very errors described in the previous section. We should not consider "the percentage of delinquents who resembled Dick when they were his age" (a mistaken frequentistic reasoning), but rather "the percentage of young men like Dick who later become delinquent" (a correct reasoning). This latter percentage may not seem high if we recall how common it is for teenagers to go through a transient, rebellious period. Most of them do not become delinquents.

To estimate such a percentage we would need to define a group similar in every respect to Dick; this would be difficult if not impossible, because of the wealth of details we know about Dick. Still, how can we assess the chance without relying completely on intuition?

As an *initial step,* we recommend temporarily ignoring some of the information we have, and concentrating on an item (or some few items) that can help us obtain an estimate of chance based on frequentistic considerations.

For example, let us deal now with the first item of information about Dick. He is a junior in a good high school in town. We can use this item to *start* to estimate Dick's chances by estimating the percentage of juniors in that high school who became entangled with the law. Perhaps this percentage is recorded at the school or by the police, but even if we cannot get this percentage, we can quite easily estimate it. The estimated percentage will be the chance of "a junior enrolled in that high school becoming entangled with the law." Still this is not *Dick's chance,* for we have not yet taken into account all the rest of the information about him.

This percentage is, then, only a *preliminary estimate* of Dick's chance of becoming entangled with the law. This is a preliminary rather than the final estimate because it concerns only a portion of the information at our disposal. The preliminary estimate uses a frequentistic consideration. This is the starting point.

Utilizing the additional information items concerning Dick, we will modify the preliminary estimate to get the final estimate. We will return to this modification later. Let us now examine ways of selecting information items for establishing a preliminary estimate by using a frequentistic approach.

Selecting Information Items for Preliminary Estimates—Some Considerations

Ted is brought to the emergency ward of the local hospital. He is 60 years old, quite fat, is complaining about acute abdominal pains, his temperature is high (102.2°), he is shuddering, and he reports dryness in his mouth.

What is the chance Ted is having an appendicitis attack?

If the doctor examining Ted wished to substantiate his diagnosis on frequentistic considerations, he would have to think about the group of people arriving in the past at the emergency ward who were 60, quite fat, complaining of abdominal pains, with high fever, shudders, and dry mouth. He should have then attempted to estimate the frequency of people having an appendicitis attack *among that group.*

This cannot be done; the group is not large enough. Nevertheless, the physician wishes to base his diagnosis partly on frequentistic considerations. If he takes our recommendation, he will *temporarily* ignore some information and will estimate the percentage of appendicitis patients out of, say, all people arriving at the emergency ward complaining about abdominal pain. He thus uses two information items: *patients coming to the emergency ward* and *patients with abdominal pains.* Or the physician could think about the percentage of appendicitis patients out of all those having both *high fever* and *abdominal pains.* The doctor has to decide what information item (or items) he will use for the preliminary estimate. How does he do that?

First, his *professional knowledge and experience* assist him in making these decisions. It is highly plausible that there are some statistics in the medical literature about the percentage of appendicitis cases among all people checked in emergency wards *having high fever.* If such statistics are not currently at his disposal, he might arrive at an estimate using his professional experience. Perhaps he feels he personally has more information concerning the percentage of appendicitis cases among those brought to the emergency ward with *abdominal pains.* If this is the case, he will start with that information.

Similarly, the school principal (Example 2) is more familiar with the percentage of those who became entangled with the law among her students than the same percentage among beer drinkers. She will, therefore, probably base her preliminary estimate on the information item "high school juniors."

Apart from the wish to start with a reasonably accurate estimate, estimators should also be guided by their assessment of the extent to which the item (items) is (are) *relevant (valid).* The school principal, for instance, may think that the critical item is the youth being a student in her school; this fact, in her view, diminishes greatly the chance of his becoming a delinquent. Thus, she will start with that item.

In contrast, a social worker who believes that amphetamine users have a high chance of becoming delinquents will probably start with the item "it is said about Dick that he takes speed." Both the school principal and the social worker will have eventually to modify their preliminary estimates according to the other information items concerning Dick.

We would expect that the two estimators will end up with similar final estimates, for they used the same data. Thus we must avoid letting the selection of the first item(s) bias the final estimate.

An estimator decides what and how many information items will be utilized for obtaining a preliminary estimate involving frequentistic considerations. Two criteria should guide the estimator.

a. A preliminary estimate should be based on an information item (or items) for which the estimator has a reasonably substantiated frequentistic estimate.

b. The starting item(s) should be most relevant (valid) regarding the matter under consideration.

10.4 FROM A PRELIMINARY ESTIMATE TO A FINAL ONE

We have reached a preliminary estimate based on a frequentistic approach: for instance, the percentage of those who become entangled with the law among all the students of a certain high school, or the percentage of appendicitis patients out of all people who report to an emergency ward with abdominal pains. How shall we proceed to consider the rest of the information?

After determining the information that will be the basis for the preliminary estimate, utilizing a frequentistic approach, we need to decide in which *direction* and to what *extent* to modify the preliminary estimate according to the additional information. We will use three guidelines for making these decisions. However, before discussing these guidelines, we ought to warn that they do not consist of exact mathematical formulas describing how much we need raise or lower the estimate. The direction and magnitude of modification will be, by and large, the result of impressions. This modification, therefore, can vary from one estimator to another.

Following are the three guidelines:

   a. Is the information new or redundant?   When we observe the items left after assessing the preliminary estimate, we ought to ask ourselves whether they are really new information or whether they are part of the information we already used. For example, supposing we learn that Dick comes from a middle-class family. Does this really single him out from the other students at the high school? If most of the students come from middle-class families, then we have, in effect, already taken this information into acount when we based our initial estimate on the student population. If, similarly, it were said of Ted that he was brought to the emergency ward feeling sick, it would not be new information; we can assume that all people who experience abdominal pain feel sick.

An item that does not add information beyond that already used for the preliminary estimate is a redundant item and should be disregarded in the transition between the preliminary estimate and the final estimate.

Hence, before deciding on modification of the preliminary estimate, we need to examine every information item for newness. If it is redundant, then we simply ought *to ignore* it.

Sometimes information is only *partially* redundant. For example, while 80% of the students at the high school have middle-class families, there are some very rich or very poor students. In that case, the information "Dick's family is middle-class" is partly redundant with the previously-used information "Dick attends X High School." To the extent that the item adds some small amount of new information, we can use it to change our estimate, but only to a small extent.

b.   Is the information reliable?   So far, we have not doubted the truthfulness of the information items we discussed.

—Dan plans to be a physician.
—Ted has acute abdominal pains.
—It is said that Dick takes amphetamines.

Such reports are not always reliable: From whom did we learn about Dan's career plans? Did those reporters know what they were talking about? Is the rumor really true about Dick's drug use? This may be a lie started by someone Dick quarreled with.

We cannot be *absolutely sure* about the truth of information based on impressions, gossip, rumors, and so on. We cannot assign such information as much weight as we would have assigned had the item been verified. If, for instance, it was Dan himself who told us that he intended to be a doctor, we would have increased our preliminary estimate based on "the percentage of those accepted into medical school among students with excellent high school grades." However, to the extent that we have doubts about the reliability of such information, we will moderate that increase.

In general, then:

> Check the reliability of every new item. To the extent that you doubt its reliability, moderate its influence on the preliminary estimate.

If reliability is important in a transition from a preliminary estimate to a final one, it is much more important in selecting the item on which the preliminary estimate will be based. The preliminary estimate has a special weight in assessing the final estimate and therefore it should be anchored to a reliable item. Before the social worker assesses a preliminary estimate for "the percentage of those becoming entangled with the law from among all amphetamine users," he ought to check whether Dick really uses amphetamines.

c. Is the item valid? The third guideline concerns the validity of every information item. The question is: should we change the preliminary estimate because of the item and to what extent?

> If the item is valid, the chances associated with the event we are trying to assess will be different when the item is true from when the item is false. If the item does not change the chances, the item is invalid.

For example, we are told that Ted is fat. Are fat people more (or less) likely to have appendicitis than non-fat people, or are the chances the same regardless of the person's weight? If the chances do not differ as weight differs, then we should disregard this item of information. If the chances do differ according to weight, the information that Ted is fat is *valid*. We will use this information to change our estimate. To do so, we need to decide whether the information *increases* or *decreases* the chances. How much should we change our estimate? That depends on our impressions of how strongly related the item is to the event we are trying to predict.

To summarize:
Every information item should be checked according to three guidelines:

a. Is it new?
b. Is it reliable?
c. Is it valid?

These guidelines will help us in shifting from a preliminary estimate (based on frequentistic considerations) to a final one. We cannot offer an accurate procedure for performing this transition, but the three guidelines should be taken into account.

The method of dealing with exceptional problems is, then:

> a. Choose one or more reliable and valid information items on which you will base a preliminary estimate, based on frequency considerations.
>
> b. Check other items for newness, reliability, and validity.
>
> c. Discard items that are completely redundant, unreliable, or invalid.
>
> d. Modify the preliminary estimate to take into account each of the remaining items. The magnitude of these modifications depends on your impression of each item's degree of newness, reliability, and validity.

10.5 CHECKING THE PROCEDURE

Much of the procedure for assessing chances involves intuitions and impressions; this is unavoidable when we deal with exceptional problems. We try to start with a solid base by using frequency considerations to determine the preliminary estimate. Still, personal impressions play a large role in the transition from a preliminary estimate to a final one. Such impressions can cause biases and mistakes. Therefore, we recommend that the final estimate be checked or reviewed, using two different methods.

Method A: Checking against your intuition.   When working through the problem, you engaged in a lengthy process with many calculations and considerations. Thus it is now appropriate to ask, does my final estimate sound reasonable? We do not recommend relying solely on one's intuition to make probability assessments for exceptional problems, but here we are recommending something slightly different: compare your final estimate with the intuitions you now hold, *after* working through the problem. To do this, use a chance wheel.

Let us suppose that after performing the whole procedure you obtain a final estimate that the chance of Dick's becoming entangled with the law is 40%. To compare this estimate against your intuitions, that is, to see if it's reasonable, you ask yourself which of the two following bets you prefer: one bet will pay $100 if, two years from now, Dick turns out to have a police record; the other bet pays $100 if, two years from now, the spinner on a chance wheel lands in the shaded area when the wheel is set at 40% shaded. (If you dislike the idea that you might profit from Dick's troubles, these bets could be written in terms of winning $100 if Dick did *not* have a police record versus winning $100 with the wheel set at 60%.) Finding yourself with a strong preference for one of these bets over the other one suggests that, intuitively, your final estimate seems wrong. Believing that these bets are approximately equally likely to pay off shows that your final estimate agrees with your intuition.

When you use this method and find that your estimate does not agree with your intuition, you should keep in mind that intuition as explored via a chance wheel is not necessarily a more valid guide to a good estimate than the starting-point-and-adjustment procedure you're checking. Just the opposite may be true. Particularly in cases with many items of information, it could happen that your global intuitive feelings are biased or that you are unable, intuitively, to make sense out of so many pieces of information at once, whereas the earlier procedure, during which you systematically sorted every item for newness, reliability, and validity and carefully considered the impact of every item in turn, would produce, in the final estimate, a better reflection of your well-reasoned beliefs. Discrepancies that occur using

Method A signal that something is wrong, but the discrepancy itself does not pinpoint the locus of the problem. You must then review all the steps you have taken to see where the problem might lie.

Checking your estimate against your intuition can be helpful in avoiding situations in which a lot of little carelessnesses or biases build up to a nonsensical final estimate. Like the first checking method used for the estimation of quantities (Chapter 5), this is a way of standing back from a final statement of chance to say "Can I really believe that?"

Method B: Using another starting point. Just as Method A is parallel to the preliminary control used for estimating quantities (see Chapter 5), so Method B is parallel to the detailed control.

Sometimes there are two different items (or sets of items), either of which could provide a solid initial estimate based on frequency considerations. When this is true, we can carry out the whole procedure twice, once with each of the two preliminary estimates.

For Dick's case, we will first start with the frequentistic estimate of the school principal, namely, "the percentage of those becoming entangled with the law out of her school's students" and modify this percentage later according to the additional information at our disposal. Setting that aside, we will start anew with "the percentage of those becoming entangled with the law among amphetamine users" (if Dick is one) and modify this preliminary estimate to take into account the other information. If we obtain two very different final estimates, it is reasonable to assume we have made mistakes in one or both procedures. But if the two final estimates are approximately equal, we feel a greater assurance that we have not made any big mistakes.

In such a way, we also control our natural inclination to overrate the items on which the preliminary estimate is based, and to underrate the additional items. We tend to *anchor* the procedure to the preliminary estimate and later change this estimate according to the other information items less than we should. For instance, if we start with a high preliminary estimate (the percentage of those becoming entangled with the law among amphetamine users) we will probably end with a higher estimated chance concerning Dick than a final estimate based on a low preliminary estimate (the percentage of those becoming entangled with the law among all the high school's students).

The fallacy of anchoring is especially severe because all of us tend to begin with a preliminary estimate that is influenced by our values. For example, the school principal hopes that Dick's chance of becoming a delinquent is low and therefore starts with the percentage of those becoming entangled with the law out of her school's students. Differences between final estimates may be the result of strong anchoring on different starting points.

By carrying out the whole procedure several times, starting at different points, we will be able to check whether there are large discrepancies between final estimates. Such discrepancies are indicative of one or more mistakes in the procedure.

Exercises for Chapter 10

1. Read the following pairs of sentences. For every sentence, please write down whether it is true or false.
   - a. 1. Most men are more than 20 years old.
        2. Most of those who are more than 20 years old are men.
   - b. 1. Most soldiers on regular military service are men.
        2. Most men are soldiers on regular military service.
   - c. 1. Most cars are private property.
        2. Most private property is cars.
   - d. 1. Most fish are not mammals.
        2. Most animals that are not mammals are fish.
   - e. 1. Most pilots also have driving licenses.
        2. Most of those who have driving licenses are pilots.
2. Choose 2 of the 4 examples from the beginning of this chapter. Please make a list of all the information items contained in each example.
   - a. Choose *one* information item that you think is suitable as a basis for a preliminary estimate. Explain your choice of that particular item.
   - b. For each one of the other items, evaluate and explain to what an extent it is:
        1. new
        2. reliable
        3. valid
   - c. For each one of these items, would you change the preliminary estimate in view of the new item, and in what direction?

11 Two Demonstrations

This final chapter presents two examples that are worked out in some detail, using the starting-point-and-adjustment method presented in Chapter 10. In the first example, we have a small amount of quite specific information that we use to form groups and subgroups. We arrive at the answer to our question by estimating the frequencies of these subgroups. In contrast, the second example provides an abundance of rather vague information. It is an exceptional problem for which it is difficult or impossible to estimate the frequencies for the relevant subgroups. Thus, in the second example we make our assessment of the chances more informally.

11.1 THE BASKETBALL PLAYER AND THE BANK PRESIDENT

Fred is a research assistant employed by a survey research institute. One day he was preparing for the computer some questionnaires filled out by a random sample of adult men in America. The questionnaires dealt with the professions and occupations of these men.

When working on one of the questionnaires, Fred saw that the respondent's occupation was marked carelessly. This is part of the questionnaire:

Respondent #423

Sex ① Male   Occupation
   2 Female

                           16   . . .
Height 1 under 5′   17 baker
        2 5′ to 5′5″   18 bank employee
        3 5′6″ to 5′11″ 19 bank president
        4 6′ to 6′5″   20 basketball player (NBA)
        ⑤ over 6′5″   21 beautician
                           22 . . .

Fred could not decide whether the respondent's occupation was bank president or basketball player. Then he noticed the respondent's height, over 6′5″. He thought, "I can't be sure, but I think there is a far greater chance this guy is a basketball player than a bank president."

The Common Approach

Most people would have estimated the chances the way Fred did. When asked to divide 100% chance between the two possibilities, they would have answered something like:

bank president   5%
basketball player 95%

The reasons for such answers would have been: "Basketball players are taller than bank presidents" or "He's tall like a basketball player." Let us now deal with this problem utilizing the techniques described in the last two chapters.

The Desirable Approach

a. A frequentistic preliminary estimate.   Let us suppose that for some reason the questionnaire under consideration lacks the information about height. In such a case we have to rely solely on the knowledge that the respondent is a male in America who is either a basketball player or a bank president. We will use frequency considerations to arrive at the chances for each occupation.

Basketball players.   A quick call to the sports desk of our local newspaper reveals that there are 23 NBA teams, each of whom carries a roster of 12 players, for a total of 276 NBA players in the United States.

Bank presidents.   We find an almanac saying that as of 1980, there were about 15,000 commercial banks in the U.S. Assuming that each bank has just one president, we can use that number as an estimate of the number of bank presidents.

Chances. Thus our respondent could be any one of 15,276 people, of whom 15,000, or 98%, are bank presidents, while 276, or 2%, are basketball players. Our preliminary estimate thus is:

bank president   98%
basketball player   2%

b. Modifying the estimate with additional information. Clearly, the information that the respondent is over 6'5" is valid—it is safe to assume that basketball players, as a group, are taller than bank presidents. And it is certainly *new* information. Let's also assume it's reliable, that the interviewer very rarely makes a mistake in filling out the questionnaire. So the respondent's height is a good piece of information we can use to change our evaluation of the chances. How can we do that? We will use that information to reduce the size of the original group, from the group of all bank presidents and basketball players to the group of only those bank presidents and basketball players who are over 6'5" (see section 9.3). With the help of the frequency table below, we will now assess the size and composition of this new reduced group.

What proportion of basketball players are over 6'5"? Many of them. Let us estimate that 60% of all basketball players are 6'6" tall or greater. That's 60% of 276 players, or 166 of them (see the table's second column).

What proportion of bank presidents are over 6'5" in height? This is a rare height for males in America. Perhaps it's a little more common among successful and prosperous males like bank presidents. Perhaps 2% of all bank presidents are over 6'5" tall. That's one in every 50; does that seem reasonable? So how many tall bank presidents are there? Two percent of 15,000 is 300 tall bank presidents (see the table's first column).

We can summarize these estimates as follows:

Frequency Table

	bank presidents	basketball players	total
6'5" or shorter	14,700	110	14,810
over 6'5"	300	166	466
Total	15,000	276	15,276

Thus, we have reduced the total group of 15,276 to a smaller group of 466 (300 + 166) that more closely matches all the information we have. Those 466 men comprise the group of males in America who are over 6'5" tall and are either bank presidents or basketball players.

Now what are the chances that the questionnaire respondent is a bank president? 300 of those 466 men are bank presidents, so the percentage is $\frac{300}{466} \times 100 = 64\%$. The rest, 36%, are basketball players. Our revised estimate, based on all our information is:

bank president   64%
basketball player   36%

c. Checking the estimate.   As recommended in the last chapter, we will check our estimate.

Method A requires us to choose between the following two bets: (1) Win $100 if the respondent is a basketball player; otherwise win nothing; and (2) Win $100 if, using a chance wheel set at 36% in the shaded area, the spinner stops in the shaded area.

Here we realize that our intuitions favor Bet 1 by a large margin. We feel that it is very likely, far more than 36% chance, that the respondent is a basketball player (we had earlier estimated the chances at 95%). Bet 1 seems *much* better than Bet 2; this shows that something is wrong.

Let us then review our procedure for possible goofs. The starting estimates came from an almanac and the sports desk of a newspaper, so they're likely to be pretty close. They also accord with our intuitions. So this doesn't seem to be the source of the problem.

Could our use of the height information be faulty? Yes, we did use rather informal and rough estimates of the proportions of bank presidents and basketball players who are over 6′5″ tall. How far off might we be? Upon reconsideration, we find it not implausible that only 1% of bank presidents (i.e., 150 of them) are that tall. And perhaps as many as 2/3 (67%) of all basketball players are that tall. Using these new estimates, we revise the frequency table to look like this:

	bank presidents	basketball players	total
6′5″ or shorter	14,850	92	14,942
over 6′5″	150	184	334
Total	15,000	276	15,276

Now our estimate for the chances that the respondent is a basketball player is $\frac{184}{334} \times 100 = 55\%$. This number is larger than our previous estimate of 36%, but it is still *much* lower than our intuitive estimate of 95%. Some fooling around with height percentages will reveal that we will get an estimate as high as 95% that the respondent is a basketball player only if we use extreme estimates like: 80% of all basketball players are over 6′5″ and only 12 out of the 15,000 bank presidents are over 6′5″. Both of these last estimates are *too* extreme. We just can't believe them. We are, therefore, convinced that our first quick and intuitive estimate (95%) was *much* too high.

We already know from Chapter 10 that intuition is not an infallible guide. Let us reexamine our intuitive estimate, and see why our intuitions mislead us. Our intuitive estimate was based on similarity: A very tall person is similar to a basketball player but not similar to a bank president. But as discussed in Chapter 10, similarity considerations can lead us astray. What our intuitive thinking omitted is revealed by our step-by-step procedures: Although very tall bank presidents are relatively unlikely, there are *so many more* bank presidents than basketball players that even the proportionately few tall ones can outnumber the tall basketball players. When we realize this, we understand why in this case it was our faulty intuition that led us astray.

Once we understand that the discrepancy revealed by checking our estimate using Method A comes from our faulty intuition and not from errors in our step-by-step procedures, we can more calmly review those procedures once again. We decide that while we're still not *certain* of the height estimates of 2% and 60% for the two occupations, they do appear to be pretty close; closer than the 1% and 67% estimates we later tried. So after all our checking (more checking than this problem may deserve, but not more checking than we ought to devote to serious life decisions), we end up feeling comfortable in saying, "The chance that our respondent is a basketball player is 36%."

Method B for checking the estimate requires us to choose some other information to use as a starting point. This method does not really apply to this simplified example. Our original question was "What are the chances the respondent is a bank president versus a basketball player?" and the question itself provided the basis for our original estimate. Gender and height, our only additional items of information, could not have been used alone to provide a starting estimate. So here we cannot use Method B.

II.2 MARRIAGE AND DIVORCE

Art: Did you hear Anne and Joe are getting married next week?

Bill: Yeah, I know Anne, but who's Joe?

Art: Oh, you know, he's that studious guy who lives down the hall; he's a junior majoring in computer science.

Cathy: You think Anne'll stay in college?

Doris: Sure, for one more year, anyway. Both their parents have agreed to support them until Joe graduates.
Bill: And if they get hard up for money, they can sell that car Anne's parents gave her last year.
Cathy: I bet that marriage won't last a year.
Bill: Why?
Cathy: Anne's such a friendly, sociable, gregarious type, while Joe's a loner—he left Sue's party last Saturday night by 9:30. They'll never get along.
Doris: Well, I heard they're getting married because Anne's pregnant.
Bill: Who told you that?
Doris: I heard two guys joking about it at Sue's party. I don't know who they were; I never saw them before.
Cathy: Juicy gossip, if true. Anybody else hear that? (pause) Anyhow, that marriage will never last; he's only 20 and she just turned 19.
Doris: Early marriages never work. Even if they make it through the first year, the chances are they'll be divorced before they can celebrate their fifth anniversary.
Art: Don't be so gloomy. They're nice, bright people. Joe'll get a good job. They'll make it.
Doris: We'll see.

From the information given above, we'll use the methods of Chapter 10 to assess the probability that Joe and Anne will still be married five years after their marriage.

a. A frequentistic preliminary estimate. First, we have to choose something to use for our starting point. Setting aside all the details about Anne and Joe, how many American marriages today last for five years? Searching the library for marriage statistics, we found relevant data only for the years 1960–1966. For those years, 93% of all marriages lasted five years or more. Can we use this statistic? Only if we believe there has been no real change since then. But we're pretty sure there has been a change since the early sixties. We've often read that divorces are more frequent today. In 1978, in America there were 2,282,000 marriages and 1,130,000 divorces. That's a lot of divorces; for every 1000 married couples at the start of 1978, there were 22 divorces during that one year alone. Of course, not all those divorces involved couples who had been married less than five years. Still, thinking hard about all we know about divorce in America today, we believe that the statistic, "93% of all marriages last for five years or more," is no longer true. After some consideration, we arrive at a lower estimate: we believe that, of all American marriages today, about 75% will last for five years or more.

Should we use this estimate of 75% as our starting point? It's certainly relevant to the problem at hand, it's simple and direct, and it provides us with a natural starting point we could adjust to take other information into account. But the trouble with this as a starting point is that it's more based on our intuitions than on any actual frequencies. Still, it's probably the best we can do. Whatever problems we encountered in arriving at the 75% estimate would still be with us were we to use some more specific fact (e.g., 5-year survival of marriages of two college students) for our starting point. So, with less confidence than we'd prefer, we'll use "75% of all U.S. marriages today survive 5 years or more" to start with.

b. Modifying the estimate with additional information.   Next we must consider the newness, validity, and reliability of each item of information.

1. Anne is 19; Joe is 20. This strikes us as new and reliable information. Furthermore, we think it's valid: we believe that divorce is more likely among those who marry when young. We definitely want to use this information.

2. Anne is friendly, sociable, gregarious; Joe is a loner, studious. Again, this seems to be new and reliable. Is it valid? Cathy thought so; she seems to believe that people who are dissimilar in outgoingness are more likely to get divorced than are similar people. But one could argue that Anne and Joe will complement each other and get along fine. After some thought, we tend to believe that personality information like this is not a valid predictor of marital success. We're going to disregard this information.

3. Anne is a freshman or sophomore in college; Joe is a junior majoring in computer science. What are we really learning here? They are college students. Are college-student marriages more stable than 19–20 year old non-student marriages? We find we can argue this both ways: intelligent and educated enough to cope with the crises that may arise, but also able to recognize when a marriage goes sour, and get out quickly. So we think there's no validity to the college-student information. How about Joe's major, computer science? That's consistent with the knowledge that Joe is a studious loner, but we already decided to disregard personality information. Finally, there's a hint here, as Art points out, that Joe's major may prepare him for a good job after graduation. This hint we will combine with two more items of information:

4. Their parents will support them until Joe graduates.

5. Anne owns a car.

Separately these items may seem irrelevant, but together they paint a picture of adequate (or better) financial support for the marriage. This derived piece of information is new, seems reasonably reliable, and valid. Young people who must scrape for money seem to us more likely to get divorced than other people. Notice here that we combined the items, "computer science major," "Joe'll get a good job," "parents' support" and "Anne's car" into a single item, "adequate financial support" in order to avoid redundancy.

6. Anne may be pregnant. If true, we might regard this as valid; a "shot-gun" marriage seems doomed. But we reject this bit of gossip as unsubstantiated and unreliable.

7. They're nice, bright people. But everybody thinks their friends are nice, and in our discussion of item 3 we already assumed they were intelligent. So there's no new information here.

What are we left with? Young people with adequate financial support. How can we use this information to alter our estimate? Perhaps we could use this information in a formal way, as we did for the bank president/basketball player example. We would create a table:

Frequency Table

	Still married after 5 years	Divorced within 5 years	Total
Young with adequate finances			
All other couples			
Total			

If we could find or estimate the frequencies for the crucial subgroups, shown boxed in the frequency table above, we could use them to assess the probability we want. But our knowledge and our almanacs now fail us. In the previous example, we could learn from an almanac that there are about 15,000 bank presidents, and our knowledge and experience with the heights of men supplied us with an estimate that about 2% of them were 6′5″ or taller. Here, however, we don't know how many marriages last five years, and our intuitions are silent on the percentage of such long-lasting marriages that involve two people who, when they got married, were young and with adequate financial support.

Instead, we will consider each fact separately. First, they are young. What are our beliefs about the effect of youth on the lastingness of marriage? We believe that people are more likely to get divorced when they marry young. Earlier, we estimated that one out of every four marriages ends in divorce within five years. But if the partners are both young, it seems to us that one out of every three will be divorced in five years. That translates into a change from our starting point of 75% to a new estimate of 67% that the marriage will last five years. Notice that even though we were unable to guess the *total* number of marriages in various subgroups, so that we couldn't fill in the frequency table, we were able to estimate a relevant *relative frequency,* one out of every three (see Chapter 9). We are approaching this problem a bit differently from the approach we used for the bank president/basketball player example, in order to make best use of what little information our intuition provides.

Next we must take account of our last fact: adequate financial support. This is a positive factor; it should increase the chances that the marriage will last. But how much should we raise our last estimate of 67%? This time our knowledge is even weaker. We don't seem to be able to estimate even relative frequencies. So we turn now to a different kind of reasoning to help us. It seems to us that the *age* factor is a stronger piece of evidence (to *lower* our estimate) than is the *financial* factor (to *raise* our estimate). So we should raise our estimate, but not as far as we just lowered it. We lowered it from 75% to 67%; now let's raise it just a little, to take into account this new but weaker information. We decide to raise it to about 70%.

We have now taken into account all the information that passed through our triple screen of new, valid, and reliable. Our final estimate is:

The chance that this marriage will last for five years is around 70%.

Checking Our Estimate

Using method A, we compare two bets:
 1. $100 won in five years if Anne and Joe are still married vs.
 2. $100 won in five years if a chance-wheel spinner lands in the 70% area.

When we think about these bets, we recognize that we feel very little confidence in the precision of our estimate. An estimate of 60% or 80% doesn't seem totally unreasonable. Still, our analysis convinces us that we disagree with Doris; the marriage seems more likely to last than to fail.

Next, let us briefly sketch an approach to Method B, checking by using a new starting point. We will take the age factor as our starting point, because we found we had strong feelings about this. But we will reword the problem to start with as low an estimate as possible, in contrast with our original analysis, which started with a rather high estimate of 75%.

Starting point.   Let us estimate the following quantity: what proportion of marriages between two people who are both younger than 21 will last, without divorce, until the death of one partner? We don't really know the answer to this question, but we feel that, eventually, most of these people will get divorced. Indeed, we believe that, of every 100 such marriages, 75 will end in divorce, whereas only 25 will endure until the death of one partner. We're not too confident in our estimate, but we'll use it as our starting point: 25% of marriages among the young last.

Adjustment 1.   We must now adjust our estimate to reflect the fact that our real interest lies in marriages that endure for five years, not forever. Of our hypothetical 100 marriages, 25 never got divorced and 75 did. When did those 75 get divorced? Early (within the first five years) or late? Again we feel quite uncertain of our estimate, but roughly, we estimate that 35 got divorced during the first five years and 40 got divorced later. So at the end of five years, 65 are still married, the 25 who will never divorce and the 40 who will get divorced later. Our new estimate is 65%.

Adjustment 2.   But our couple's ages are not 15 and 16, they're near the top of the age range, 19 and 20. That's a positive sign; we use it to increase the chances from 65% to 70%.

Adjustment 3.   The financial factor is also, in our minds, positive. We use it to raise our estimate again, from 70% to 75%.

Because we have now used all the valid, new reliable information, this is our final estimate: 75%. This doesn't differ much from our original estimate of 70%. We realize that our recalculations were even more subjective and open to error than was our original analysis. We conclude that our estimate is only approximate. Still, these analyses have made us reasonably confident that Anne and Joe's chances are fairly high, perhaps somewhere in the range 60% to 85%.

11.3 FINAL COMMENT

While the two problems discussed in this chapter may seem trivial, we believe they capture some essential aspects of the serious, important problems involving uncertainty that one encounters:

1. Research or consultations with experts will often reveal highly relevant estimates.

2. But one's own problem (particularly exceptional problems) will have special features for which no solid facts are available. One inevitably ends up relying to some extent on subjective beliefs.

3. A careful analysis will enable one to merge the "hard facts" with the "soft impressions," thus yielding a better estimate than would reliance on either the facts alone or unaided intuition.

4. We should choose a structure for our analysis that is most compatible with the form of our facts and beliefs.

Exercises for Chapter 11

1. Reread the basketball player/bank president analysis. Is there any estimate you feel is wrong? If so, make a new estimate (or more, as needed)

and complete the calculations with your new estimates. Is bank president still the more likely answer?

2. Repeat the entire marriage/divorce example, making your own judgments about starting point, newness, validity, reliability, and adjustments. Would you rather bet on divorce or no divorce after five years?

3. Choose a problem that interests you and for which you feel you have some information. Analyze it using a starting point and appropriate modifications. Check it afterwards.

Bibliography and Background Reading

General

Behn, R. D., & Vaupel, J. W. *Quick analysis for busy decision makers.* New York: Basic Books, 1982.

Detmer, D. E., Fryback, D. G., & Gassner, K. Heuristics and biases in medical decision making. *Journal of Medical Education,* 1978, *53,* 682–683.

Einhorn, H. J. Decision errors and fallible judgment: Implications for social policy. In K. R. Hammond (Ed.), *Judgment and decision in public policy formation.* Denver: Westview Press, 1978.

Einhorn, H. J., & Hogarth, R. M. Behavioral decision theory: Processes of judgment and choice. *Annual Review of Psychology,* 1981, *32,* 53–88.

Edwards, W., Lindman, H., & Savage, L. J. Bayesian statistical inference for psychological research. *Psychological Review,* 1963, *70,* 193–242.

Feller, W. An introduction to probability theory and its application. New York: Wiley, 1950.

Fischhoff, B., & Beyth-Marom, R. Hypothesis evaluation from a Bayesian perspective. *Psychological Review,* 1983, *90,* 239–260.

Fischhoff, B., Lichtenstein, S., Slovic, P., Derby, S. L., & Keeney, R. L. *Acceptable risk.* New York: Cambridge University Press, 1981.

Fischhoff, B., Svenson, O., & Slovic, P. Active responses to environmental hazards. In D. Stokols & I. Altman (Eds.), *Handbook of environmental psychology.* New York: Wiley, in press.

Hogarth, R. M. *Judgment and choice: The psychology of decision.* Chichester, England: Wiley, 1980.

Janis, I. L., & Mann, L. *Decision making: A psychological analysis of conflict, choice, and commitment.* New York: Macmillan, 1977.

Kahneman, D., Slovic, P., & Tversky, A. (Eds.). *Judgment under uncertainty: Heuristics and biases.* New York: Cambridge University Press, 1982.

Kahneman, D., & Tversky, A. On the study of statistical intuitions. In D. Kahneman, P. Slovic, & A. Tversky (Eds.), *Judgment under uncertainty: Heuristics and biases.* New York: Cambridge University Press, 1982.

Nisbett, R. E., & Ross, L. *Human inference: Strategies and shortcomings of social judgments.* Englewood Cliffs, N.J.: Prentice-Hall, 1980.

Raiffa, H. *Decision analysis.* Reading, Mass.: Addison-Wesley, 1968.

Savage, L. J. *The foundations of statistics.* New York: Wiley, 1954.

Shelly, M. W. II, & Bryan, G. L. *Human judgments and optimality.* New York: Wiley, 1964.

Slovic, P., Fischhoff, B., & Lichtenstein, S. Behavioral decision theory. *Annual Review of Psychology,* 1977, *28,* 1–39.

Slovic, P., Lichtenstein, S., & Fischhoff, B. Decision making. In R. C. Atkinson, R. J. Herrnstein, G. Lindzey, & R. D. Luce (Eds.), *Stevens' Handbook of Experimental Psychology* (2nd ed.). New York: Wiley, in press.

Tversky, A., & Kahneman, D. Judgment under uncertainty: Heuristics and biases. In D. Kahneman, P. Slovic, & A. Tversky (Eds.), *Judgment under uncertainty: Heuristics and biases.* New York: Cambridge University Press, 1982.

Ungson, G. R., & Braunstein, D. N. (Eds.). *Decision making: An interdisciplinary inquiry.* Boston: Kent, 1982.

Section 1: Chapters 1–4

Beyth-Marom, R. How probable is probable? Numerical translation of verbal probability expressions. *Journal of Forecasting,* 1982, *1,* 247–269.

Coombs, C. H., Dawes, R. M., & Tversky, A. *Mathematical psychology: An elementary introduction.* Chapter 10, Information theory. Englewood Cliffs, N.J.: Prentice-Hall, 1970.

Fischhoff, B., Slovic, P., & Lichtenstein, S. Fault trees: Sensitivity of estimated failure probabilities to problem representation. *Journal of Experimental Psychology: Human Perception and Performance,* 1978, *4,* 330–344.

Kahneman, D., & Tversky, A. Variants of uncertainty. In D. Kahneman, P. Slovic, and A. Tversky (Eds.), *Judgment under uncertainty: Heuristics and biases.* New York: Cambridge University Press, 1982.

Lichtenstein, S., & Newman, J. R. Empirical scaling of common verbal phrases associated with numerical probabilities. *Psychonomic Science,* 1967, *9,* 563–564.

Murphy, A. H., & Winkler, R. L. Subjective probability forecasting experiments in meteorology. Some preliminary results. *Bulletin of the American Meteorological Society,* 1974, *55,* 1206–1216.

Oskamp, S. Overconfidence in case-study judgments. *Journal of Consulting Psychology,* 1965, *29,* 261–265.

Savage, L. J. Elicitation of personal probabilities and expectations. *Journal of the American Statistical Association,* 1971, *66*(336), 783–801.

Slovic, P. Value as a determiner of subjective probability. *Transactions of the Institute of Electronic Engineers: Human Factors Issue,* 1966, *HFE-7,* 22–28.

Wallsten, T., & Budescu, D. Encoding subjective probabilities: A psychological and psychometric review. *Management Science,* 1983, *29,* 151–173.

Section 2: Chapters 5–7

Armstrong, J. S., Denniston, W. B. Jr., & Gordon, M. M. The use of the decomposition principle in making judgments. *Organizational Behavior and Human Performance,* 1975, *14,* 257–263.

Bar-Hillel, M. The role of sample size in sample evaluation. *Organizational Behavior and Human Performance,* 1979, *24,* 245–257.

Beyth-Marom, R. Perception of correlation reexamined. *Memory and Cognition,* 1982, *10,* 511–519.

Combs, B., & Slovic, P. Causes of death: Biased newspaper coverage and biased judgments. *Journalism Quarterly,* 1979, *56,* 837–843, 849.

Goodman, S. E., & Hedethiemi, S. T. *Introduction to the design and analysis of algorithms.* New York: McGraw-Hill, 1977.

Kahneman, D., & Tversky, A. Availability and the simulation heuristic. In D. Kahneman, P. Slovic, & A. Tversky (Eds.), *Judgment under uncertainty: Heuristics and biases.* New York: Cambridge University Press, 1982.

Lichtenstein, S., Slovic, P., Fischhoff, B., Layman, M., & Combs, B. Judged frequency of lethal events. *Journal of Experimental Psychology: Human Learning and Memory,* 1978, *4,* 551–578.

Peters, J. T., Hammond, K. K., & Summers, D. A. A note on intuitive vs. analytic thinking. *Organizational Behavior and Human Performance,* 1974, *12,* 125–131.

Taylor, S. E. The availability bias in social perception and interaction. In D. Kahneman, P. Slovic, & A. Tversky (Eds.), *Judgment under uncertainty: Heuristics and biases.* New York: Cambridge University Press, 1982.

Tversky, A., & Kahneman, D. The belief in the "law of small numbers." *Psychological Bulletin,* 1971, *76,* 105–110.

Tversky, A., & Kahneman, D. Availability: A heuristic for judging frequency and probability. *Cognitive Psychology,* 1973, *4,* 207–232.

Section 3: Chapters 8–11

Bar-Hillel, M. The base rate fallacy in probability judgments. *Acta Psychologica,* 1980, *44,* 211–233.

Bar-Hillel, M. Similarity and probability. *Organizational Behavior and Human Performance,* 1974, *11,* 277–282.

Bar-Hillel, M., & Fischhoff, B. When do base rates affect predictions? *Journal of Personality and Social Psychology,* 1981, *41,* 671–680.

Eddy, D. M. Probabilistic reasoning in clinical medicine: Problems and opportunities. In D. Kahneman, P. Slovic, & A. Tversky (Eds.), *Judgment under uncertainty: Heuristics and biases.* New York: Cambridge University Press, 1982.

Edwards, W. Conservatism in human information processing. In D. Kahneman, P. Slovic, & A. Tversky (Eds.), *Judgment under uncertainty: Heuristics and biases.* New York: Cambridge University Press, 1982.

Fischhoff, B. Debiasing. In D. Kahneman, P. Slovic, & A. Tversky (Eds.), *Judgment under uncertainty: Heuristics and biases.* New York: Cambridge University Press, 1982, 422–444.

Fischhoff, B., & Bar-Hillel, M. Diagnosticity and the base rate effect. *Memory and Cognition,* in press.

Fischhoff, B., & Bar-Hillel, M. Focusing techniques: A shortcut to improving probability judgments? *Organizational Behavior and Human Performance,* in press.

Fischhoff, B., Slovic, P., & Lichtenstein, S. Subjective sensitivity analysis. *Organizational Behavior and Human Performance,* 1979, *23,* 339–359.

Kahneman, D., & Tversky, A. Subjective probability: A judgment of representativeness. *Cognitive Psychology,* 1972, *3,* 430–454.

Kahneman, D., & Tversky, A. On the psychology of prediction. *Psychological Review,* 1973, *80,* 237–251.

Kahneman, D., & Tversky, A. Intuitive prediction: Biases and corrective procedures. *TIMS Studies in Management Science,* 1979, *12,* 313–327.

Solomon, W. C. *The foundations of scientific inference.* Pittsburgh, Pennsylvania: University of Pittsburgh Press, 1966.

Subject Index